C000071929

Landscapes of
CORFU

a countryside guide
Third edition

Noel Rochford

SUNFLOWER BOOKS

Dedicated to Dorina

Revised printing 2000
Third edition 1999
by Sunflower Books™
12 Kendrick Mews
London SW7 3HG, UK

ISBN 1-85691-135-7

Episkepsis (Walk 6)

Important note to the reader _____

We have tried to ensure that the descriptions and maps in this book are error-free at press date. It will be very helpful for us to receive your comments (sent in care of the publishers, please) for the updating of future printings.

　　We also rely on those who use this book — especially walkers — to take along a good supply of common sense when they explore. Conditions change fairly rapidly on Corfu, and **storm damage or bulldozing may make a route unsafe at any time**. If the route is not as we outline it here, and your way ahead is not secure, return to the point of departure. **Never attempt to complete a tour or walk under hazardous conditions!** Please read carefully the notes on pages 17 and 41 to 46, as well as the introductory comments at the beginning of each tour and walk (regarding road conditions, equipment, grade, distances and time, etc). Explore **safely**, while at the same time respecting the beauty of the countryside.

Cover photograph: Coastline near Nissaki
Title page: Pondikonisi (Mouse Island)

Photographs by the author
Maps by John Underwood
Drawings by Sharon Rochford
A CIP catalogue record for this book is available from the British
　Library.
Printed and bound in Great Britain by J. H. Haynes & Co Ltd.

10 9 8 7 6 5 4 3

Contents

Vegetable plots and olive groves outside Paleochori (Walk 21 and Car tour 4)

❀ Preface

For centuries Corfu's magnetic beauty has attracted travellers, who have sung the praises of the peacock-hued bays, the hillsides drenched in silvery-green olive trees, and the emerald greenness of the countryside. And when you leave Corfu, these will be your impressions too. While time brings change, the pristine Corfu so beloved of Lear and the Durrell brothers can still be found, and this book tells you where. It turns the island inside-out and helps you find a Corfu unknown to most tourists.

The book focuses on walking, but it is not intended *only* for walkers. The car touring section will show you the best of the island, and the picnic suggestions make an excellent introduction to the countryside — many of them being at exhilarating viewpoints, reached after only a very short, leg-stretching walk from your touring route. You just might be tempted to return another day and explore a bit further.

Walking on Corfu is sheer bliss. You will be spoilt by a kaleidoscope of landscapes, and you needn't be an intrepid hiker to find these beauty spots. The walks lead to some of the most beautiful beaches you'll ever see, from the secluded pebbly coves of the northwest to the pellucid horseshoe bay of Ag Georgiou, the sand dunes of the Korission Lagoon and Durrell's favourite, Mirtiotissa. If you're adventurous, the rugged goat country of Mount Pantokrator will appeal to you. For strolls and short rambles, meander over the silvan hills or cross vast grassy plains flecked with flowers, surprise terrapin sunbasking in muddy ponds, plough through Corfu's few remaining holly oak woods, step across silently-flowing streams, and — in the bleaker corners of the island — listen to the echoes of abandoned villages.

In spring and autumn Corfu is at its best — alight with a spectacle of wild flowers that cover the colour spectrum. The fields and slopes are splashed with violet-blue Venus' looking-glass, flesh-pink geraniums, mauve anemones, vivid yellow marigolds, carmine cyclamen, creamy crocuses, sunflower-yellow *Sternbergia*, and elaborately-marked orchids. Even the thistles contribute to this floral splendour. And for fun, there's the squirting cucumber — touch it and see what happens!

Trees are another part of this finely-embroidered landscape. Perhaps the most eye-catching is the Judas tree in spring, with its dangling clusters of purple florets. In the country, massive oaks and twirling turpentine trees shade solitary dwellings and churches. Everywhere, the dark spires of the cypress pierce the island's cloak of olives.

Corfu has suffered a turbulent history of occupations and invasions — most recently the invasion of tourists. For four months of the year, the island is besieged by great hordes of them. This is the side of Corfu that you *don't* want to see. To know Corfu is to know the people. Out in the country is where you're more likely to experience the real friendliness — provided that *you* make the first move. So if you speak a smattering of Greek, don't hestitate to do so. The rewards will be immense. This is the Corfu of Lear and the Durrells. Taste the untainted rawness in the country, and not the synthetic spillage that follows tourism everywhere. There are today two Corfus and, with the help of *Landscapes of Corfu*, I hope you find the real island.

Acknowledgements

A very special thanks to Corfu Villas for the use of 'Petunia', a magnificently-sited villa, for the duration of my ground work.

Heartfelt thanks to David Baker, for his Herculean efforts in re-walking all the routes for the previous edition of this book.

Many thanks to the 'tremendous trio' on Corfu, who helped me with the first edition: Anne Nash, who showed me the flowers and quiet countryside, identified so many plants, and answered endless questions; Aleco Damaskinos, who accompanied me on walks, giving suggestions, help, and many laughs; Christopher Lavranos who, if he did not know the answers to my questions, always knew someone who did.

Thanks also to Maria Aspiotti, George Manessis and Costas Alamanos for information about the island; the Greek Tourist Office; Mr and Mrs Pagratis for their kindness; the Reading Society of Corfu; my sister Sharon for her excellent drawings; my parents, friends and publisher, for their continued support.

Recommended books

Landscapes of Corfu is a *countryside guide,* and it cannot be emphasised too strongly that it should be used in tandem with a good standard guide, of which there are several available. As a field guide to the island's flora I have used Huxley and Taylor, *Flowers of Greece* (Chatto, 1984; available from libraries) and three books by George Sfikas (available on Corfu): *Wild Flowers of Greece, Trees and Shrubs of Greece,* and *Medicinal Plants of Greece.* Finally, for background reading, seek out the latest paperback editions of Lawrence Durrell's *Prospero's Cell* and Gerald Durrell's *My Family and Other Animals.*

☀ Getting about _____

The two most popular and affordable ways of getting about on Corfu are by bus and rented transport. Even though the bus network is fairly extensive, it's not always convenient for walks and picnics. During peak season the buses are jam-packed and so sometimes do not call at intermediate bus stops, as they cannot take on any more passengers. And they often run late. For these reasons, renting a vehicle is a good option.

Car rental on the island is fairly expensive, and you will pay a lower price if you book and pay in advance, either with your tour operator or one of the lower-price international car hire firms with agents on the island. **Scooter** and **bike rental**, however, is very economical and one of the most popular ways of getting about.

Coach excursions allow you to see all the major sights in comfort, but they provide no opportunity for contact with countryside life. **Taxis** are another alternative, and sharing with others will help cut costs. Always agree on a price before setting out, and don't be afraid to do a little good-natured bargaining.

Outside the main tourist resorts, the **local bus** network* (see timetables pages 128-134) serves the local populace, not the visitor. This means that buses leave Corfu Town for far-flung villages very early in the morning and return mid-afternoon. Many of the walks described end along these countryside bus routes. To catch the day's only return bus means galloping through some walks — not everyone's idea of a pleasant hike. The problem is exaggerated as the season tails off, when late afternoon buses from some resorts are discontinued. One way to overcome this problem is to stay overnight where your walk ends, which is not difficult outside July/August, since there are rooms for rent all over the island. Otherwise, you must arrange for friends or a taxi to collect you. Cars and bikes can also be used in tandem with the bus services, by leaving your car at either the beginning or end of the walk and taking a bus in the other direction.

*See notes about buses and bus stations in the timetables on page 128; bus stations are shown on the town plan overleaf.

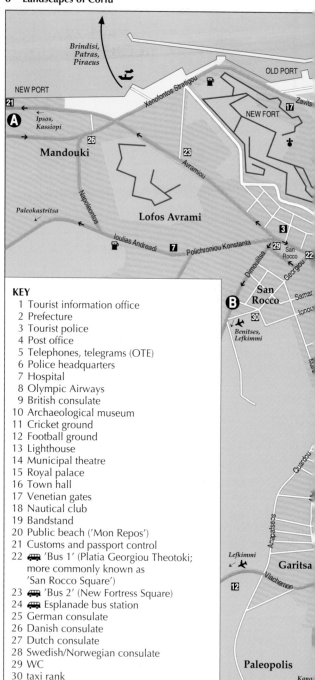

NEW PORT

OLD PORT

Brindisi,
Patras,
Piraeus

Xenofontos Stratigou

NEW FORT

Zavits

A

21

← *Ipsos,*
Kassiopi

26

23

Avramiou

17

Mandouki

Napoleontos

Paleokastritsa
←

Ioulias Andreadi   7   Polichroniou Konstanta

Lofos Avrami

Dimoulitsa

San
Rocco

Georgiou

29

3

22

B

**San
Rocco**

Samar

Ionou

30

← ✈
Benitses,
Lefkimmi

Quardou

Lefkimmi
← ✈

Garitsa

12

Anapatsens

Vlachernon

Paleopolis

Kano

KEY
1 Tourist information office
2 Prefecture
3 Tourist police
4 Post office
5 Telephones, telegrams (OTE)
6 Police headquarters
7 Hospital
8 Olympic Airways
9 British consulate
10 Archaeological museum
11 Cricket ground
12 Football ground
13 Lighthouse
14 Municipal theatre
15 Royal palace
16 Town hall
17 Venetian gates
18 Nautical club
19 Bandstand
20 Public beach ('Mon Repos')
21 Customs and passport control
22 🚌 'Bus 1' (Platia Georgiou Theotoki;
    more commonly known as
    'San Rocco Square')
23 🚌 'Bus 2' (New Fortress Square)
24 🚌 Esplanade bus station
25 German consulate
26 Danish consulate
27 Dutch consulate
28 Swedish/Norwegian consulate
29 WC
30 taxi rank

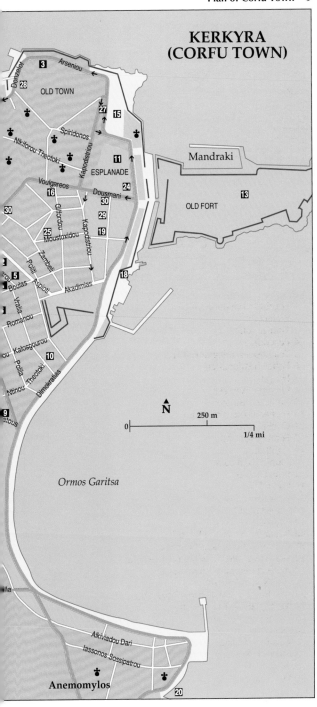

KERKYRA
(CORFU TOWN)

❋ Picnicking

Corfu abounds in scenic little corners, many of which make ideal picnic spots. Ideal because they're far from the madding crowd, and unspoilt. They give you a feel for the countryside, yet you don't have to hike for miles. All my picnic suggestions are within easy reach, and most can be extended into short walks, should your curiosity get the better of you. There are no public picnic sites on the island, and none of my suggestions offers anything more than a lovely setting or a superb view. There are landscapes to suit all tastes — secluded coves, mountaintops, lagoons, olive groves, grassy fields, and abandoned monasteries.

All the information you need to get to these picnic spots is given on the following pages, where picnic numbers correspond to walk numbers, so that you can quickly find the general location on the island by looking at the large touring map (where the walks are shown in green). I include transport details (🚌: how to get there by bus; 🚗: where to leave your private trans-

port), how long a walk you'll have, and views or setting. Beside the picnic title, you'll find a map reference: the location of the picnic spot is shown on this walking map by the symbol **P** printed in green; 🚌 and 🚐 symbols indicate where to leave your transport. Some of the picnic settings are illustrated.

Please glance over the comments before you start off on your picnic: if more than a few minutes' walking is required, remember to wear sensible shoes and to **take a sunhat** (○ indicates a picnic **in full sun**). It's a good idea to take along a plastic groundsheet as well, in case the ground is damp (or prickly).

If you're travelling to your picnic by bus, be sure to update the timetables at the back of this book (pages 128-134), preferably by making enquiries at the bus stations. Remember that the timetables given in this book are for high season only and subject to change.

If you are travelling to your picnic by private transport, be extra vigilant off the main roads: children and animals are often on the village streets. Without damaging plants, park *well off* the roadside; never block a road or track!

All picnickers should read the country code on page 17 and go quietly in the countryside.

You have two choices for Picnic 11 on Cape Arilla. Either follow Short walk 11 (page 86) to this splendid view over the twin coves of Port Timone or, to enjoy a view north to Gravia Island and Cape Ag Stefanos, take the wide footpath opposite the front door of the church at Afionas. Up amidst the houses, take the second alley on the left, followed by a right and then another left. This path follows the spine of the ridge to the 'donkey parking lot'; there are usually a few donkeys here, munching straw — it makes a terrific photo. Continue on the path for another five minutes, ascending the rocky hillock over to the right.

You needn't be a picnicker to enjoy my suggestions; they make perfect 'leg stretchers', a good way to break up a tour and visit places the casual tourist never sees.

But if you *are* going to have a picnic, make it one to remember! Here's a short recipe for a healthy picnic: fresh fruit from the market, *angouria* (cucumbers), *domades* (tomatoes), a slab of *feta* (cheese), *mortadella* (a garlicky sausage), some *taramosalata* and *tzatziki* from the supermarket, some fleshy maroon olives (if you're into olives). Then pick up a loaf or two of fresh village bread en route. If you have a sweet tooth, add *baklava* (a pastry filled with nuts and oozing honey) or *rizogala* (cold rice pudding). Don't forget the wine!

1 AG SPIRIDON (map page 47, photograph page 48) ○

by car: 20-30min on foot   *by bus: about 1h on foot*
🚗 Ag Spiridon Beach, northeast of Kassiopi. (Car tour 1)
🚌 Kassiopi/Roda bus to the Nea Perithia/Loutses turn-off.
Either follow Walk 1 (page 47) to the first cove beyond the main beach and picnic anywhere over the bridge, or take the track cutting across the headland past the old monastery, to the estuary shown on page 48. No shade.

2 IMEROLIA (map: reverse of touring map, photograph page 52)

by car: 10-20min on foot   *by bus: 10-20min on foot.*
🚗 Imerolia, at the roadside (1km north of Kassiopi). (Car tour 1)
🚌 Kassiopi/Roda bus to Imerolia.

Either follow Walk 2 (page 50), to picnic on the shady flower-filled path shown on page 52 or, for fine views across the bay (but no shade), start at the school at the northern end of the bay. Walk along the drive to the school for a few metres/yards, then turn left on a gravel track. Just below the second house, turn right on a path and follow it up the ridge as far as you like

Olive groves are pleasant picnic spots. This photograph was taken 20 minutes below Episkepsis, on Walk 6.

3 NISSAKI (map on reverse of touring map)

by car: 10-40min on foot   *by bus: 10-40min on foot*
🚗 Nissaki, off the main road, west of the Club Med *(room for one or two cars only)*. (Car tour 1)
🚌 to Nissaki; get off at the Club Med.
See notes on page 53 to start Walk 3. Picnic anywhere beyond the houses, under the shade of olive trees. Above the village of Katavolos there are stunning sea views over the Gulf of Kerkyra and Albania.

4a NEAR THE NISSAKI BEACH HOTEL (map on reverse of touring map, photographs pages 58-59 and cover)

by car: 10-15min on foot   *by bus: 10-15min on foot*
🚗 Nissaki Beach Hotel car park. (Car tour 1)
🚌 to Nissaki Beach Hotel turn-off (Kassiopi bus).
From the beach below the hotel, head either left or right along the coast, following footpaths along the stupendously-beautiful rocky shoreline. Shade of olive trees. Walk 4 follows this route.

4b KALAMI (map on reverse of touring map, photograph page 60)

by car: 15-20min on foot   *by bus: 25-30min on foot*
🚗 Kalami Beach; the turn-off is north of Nissaki. (Car tour 1)
🚌 to the Kalami/Kouloura junction (Kassiopi bus).
From the bus stop head down to Kalami Beach. Walk along the beach and take the path beside the restaurant at end of the beach, back up to the Kalami road. Lawrence Durrell lived in the restaurant building here when he wrote *Prospero's Cell*. Follow the road up the hill, then fork left on a track. When the track ends, continue on a path, to the exquisite cove below. Shade from a few olive trees.

4c KOULOURA (map on reverse of touring map)

by car: up to 5min on foot   *by bus: 10-15min on foot*
🚗 seafront at Kouloura. The turn-off is north of Nissaki; keep left and take the first gravel track down to the beach. (Car tour 1)
🚌 to the Kalami/Kouloura junction (Kassiopi bus). Follow the directions for motorists to reach the beach.
This is a pretty, unspoilt pebble beach, with shade from tall eucalyptus trees.

5 ANO PERITHIA (map on reverse of touring map, photographs pages 62-63, 64, 74)

by car: 5-10min on foot   *by bus: not accessible*
🚗 near the church above Ano Perithia. (Car tour 1)
Head down into the village square, pass to the left of the two restaurants, and follow the footpath to explore the rest of the village and find a quiet corner. Shade of trees or abandoned buildings. You can also use the notes in Walk 5 (from the 4h20min-point, page 64), to follow the track some of the way to Lafki and back.

6 STRINILAS (map on reverse of touring map) ○

by car: 10-15min on foot   *by bus: scheduling unsuitable*
🚗 Strinilas, in the parking area on the north side of the village. (Car tour 1)
Descending from the village square towards Spartilas, turn right down a concrete lane just past the Strinilas sign. At the T-junction 30m/yds ahead, turn left down a track. Head over to the crest, where you have encompassing views over the northern hills and an enclosed valley below. Particularly pleasant in spring and autumn, but little shade.

7 SPARTILAS (map on reverse of touring map)

by car: up to 10min on foot   *by bus: scheduling unsuitable*

🚗 Spartilas village, on narrow streets. Don't block traffic! (Car tour 1)
🚌 to Spartilas.

Follow the start of Walk 7 (page 71). Picnic anywhere in the olive grove off the road, minutes above the village. For views over Ipsos Bay, you'll need to climb the overgrown hillside. Shade of olive trees

8 NIMFES (map on reverse of touring map; photograph page 77)

by car: 15-20min on foot   *by bus: scheduling unsuitable*

🚗 Nimfes. (Car tour 2)

Follow Walk 8 (page 76) to reach the abandoned monastery of Pantokrator, ensconced in a cypress wood. It's wonderfully quiet here.

9 TROUMPETA PASS (map on reverse of touring map) ○

by car: 15-25min on foot   *by bus: 15-25min on foot*

🚗 Troumpeta (limited parking). (Car tours 2 and 3)
🚌 Sidari/Roda bus; alight at Troumpeta, the pass you cross en route to Sidari and Roda.

As you approach Troumpeta from the south, a gravel track branches off to the right at the beginning of the hamlet at the pass. Follow it uphill as far as you like; there are good views over the central hills early on. After a climb of 15 minutes, you can see the north of the island. No shade, so this is *not* a picnic spot recommended for high summer.

11 CAPE ARILLA FROM AFIONAS (map pages 86-87; nearby photographs pages 10-11, 27)

by car: 10-15min on foot   *by bus: scheduling unsuitable*

🚗 Afionas. The bus turns round here, in the square, so park off the side of the road at least 100m below the square. (Car tour 2)

See notes beside the photograph on pages 10-11.

12a MT ARAKLI (map pages 86-87, photograph pages 18-19)

by car: 15-25min on foot   *by bus: scheduling unsuitable*

🚗 Lakones (the signposted turn-off is northeast of Paleokastritsa). The road is narrow; don't block through traffic. (Car tour 3)

For the best possible view over the famous Liapades Bay, follow Walk 12 from the 40min-point (page 90), climbing as far as you like. Shade of olive trees nearby.

12b AG GEORGIOS BEACH (map pages 86-87) ○

by car: 15-20min on foot   *by bus: 15-20min on foot*

🚗 Ag Georgios Beach (via Pagi, off the Sidari road). (Car tour 2)
🚌 to Ag Georgios.

Head left (south) along the track behind the beach, continuing as far as you like. Paths lead off from the track to beautiful, secluded sandy beaches. Shade of olive groves nearby.

12c ANGELOKASTRO (map pages 86-87)

by car: 5-10min on foot   *by bus: scheduling unsuitable*

🚗 Angelokastro car park, below the castle. (Car tour 3)

The best place to picnic is in the olive groves on the hill opposite the castle. A path ascending from the car park towards Krini climbs up beside these groves. Shade

The sand dunes near Issos Beach, with Mt Ag Mattheos in the background (Picnic 20, Walk 20, Car tour 4)

13 NEAR GAVROLIMNI POND (map pages 100-101)

by car: 15-20min on foot   *by bus: not easily accessible*

🚗 Ropa Plain, at the side of a track. Crossing the Ropa Plain from Liapades, heading south, turn left on a lane where there is a grasshopper sign (see Car tour 3, page 32). Half a kilometre along, the lane reverts to gravel, and 100m further on there is a lay-by for cars alongside the track.

Use the map on pages 100-101 to explore the plain and visit the ponds. This is a beautiful, peaceful pastureland setting, as can be seen in the photograph on pages 32-33. Plenty of shade in this lush valley.

14 DOUKADES (map pages 100-101, photograph page 102)

by car: 15-40min on foot   *by bus: not easily accessible*

🚗 Doukades; park in the square. (Car tour 3)

Walk back along the road towards Paleokastritsa, then take the first alley on the right, to pass a church on your right. Now pick up the notes on page 102, to follow Walk 14 from the 3h-point, climbing the escarpment behind Doukades. There is a fine countryside panorama of the central hills after 10 minutes' climbing. Shade of olive trees. A 40-minute climb leads to the beautifully-sited chapel of Ag Simeon shown on page 102, but there is little shade up there.

15 MIRTIOTISSA BEACH (map pages 108-109; photograph pages 106-107) ○

by car: 15-20min on foot   *by bus: 25-35min on foot*

🚗 above Mirtiotissa Beach. The turn-off is 3km south of Vatos. About 0.5km down the track to the beach, park in a hollow shaded by olive trees. (Car tour 3)

🚌 to the Mirtiotissa Beach turn-off (Glyfada bus).

Follow the very steep gravelly track down to the beach. The return is a real slog! Note: this is a naturist beach.

16 BENITSES (map page 113)

by car: 20-30min on foot   *by bus: 20-30min on foot*

🚗 Benitses (Car tour 4). After parking, walk on to the bus stop/shelter by the jetty.

🚌 to Benitses

Just opposite the bus stop/shelter — across the island square — an alley heads back into the houses. Follow it, using the map on page 113 to reach the waterworks. Choose your spot after passing through the archway (about 15min up the valley). This lush, overgrown garden is shaded by thick foliage. It's an intoxicating spot!

17 DAFNATA (map page 113)

by car: 5-10min on foot	*by bus: 5-10min on foot*

🚗 Dafnata. The turn off is between Strongili and Gastouri, on the alternative route for Car tour 4 (page 35).

🚌 to Dafnata (Strongili bus).

There are two possiblities. For *views,* take the path that climbs above Dafnata: follow Walk 17 from the 1h15min-point (page 115). For *bucolic charm,* take the path that descends from the village: follow Walk 17 from the 2h35min-point (page 116). Shade in both spots.

18a HLOMOS (map pages 118-119, photograph page 117)

by car: 5-10min on foot	*by bus: 5-10min on foot*

🚗 Hlomos, 5.5km south of the Messongi junction. (Car tour 4)

🚌 bus to Hlomos

Head into the village from the bus shelter/car parking area. Take the path ascending to the left, signposted for the church.

18b KORAKADES (map pages 118-119)

by car: 5-10min on foot	*by bus: scheduling unsuitable*

🚗 outside Korakades, at the end of the asphalt road, in a turning area. Leave the main south road in Argirades, following signs for Petreti and Kouspades. Keep left at the Petreti junction and right at the Kouspades junction. Continue until the road ends. (Car tour 4)

Head through Korakades and follow the lane leading out on the other side. Five minutes along you'll come to some abandoned houses. There's a tremendous outlook from here, over the rooftops onto the Lefkimmi flats and the hills of Epirus. You can sit on the wall on the side of the road, in the shade of olive trees.

18c PETRETI (map pages 118-119)

by car: 10-15min on foot	*by bus: scheduling unsuitable*

🚗 Petreti, either by the port or near the beach. (Car tour 4)

Walk south along the shore, cross two streams, then follow the path up and over the hill to the next cove, called Notos. A quiet, little-frequented spot. Shade of olive trees nearby.

20a KORISSION LAGOON (map page 122) ○

by car: up to 5min on foot	*by bus: not easily accessible*

🚗 Mesavrisi. Turn off for Gardiki Castle (south of Ag Mattheos). Go left at the first junction, then go left again, following the signs for Mesavrisi.

Picnic anywhere by the lagoon. No shade

20b ISSOS BEACH (map pages 118-119, photograph page 15) ○

by car: up to 15min on foot	*by bus: not easily accessible*

🚗 Issos Beach. The turn-off is in Linia, 5.5km south of the Ano Messongi junction on the main south road, just beyond a petrol station. (Car tour 4)

You can picnic in sand dunes, overlooking the lagoon and an un-touched stretch of coastline. No shade.

A country code for walkers and motorists

The experienced rambler is used to following a 'country code', but the tourist out for a lark may unwittingly cause damage, harm animals, and even endanger his own life. Do heed this advice:

- **Do not light fires.** Stub out all cigarettes.
- **Do not frighten animals.** The goats and sheep you may encounter on your walks are not tame. By making loud noises or trying to touch or photograph them, you may cause them to run in fear and be hurt.
- **Walk quietly** through all farms, hamlets and villages, leaving all gates just as you found them. Gates do have a purpose, usually to keep animals in — or out of — an area.
- **Protect all wild and cultivated plants.** Don't try to pick wild flowers or uproot saplings. Obviously fruit and crops are someone's private property and should not be touched.
- **Never** walk over cultivated land.
- **Take all your litter away with you.**
- **Do not take risks.** Do not attempt walks beyond your capacity and *never* walk alone. Always tell a responsible person exactly where you are going and what time you plan to return. Remember, if you become lost or injure yourself, it may be a long time before you are found. On any but a very short walk near villages, it's a good idea to take along a torch and a whistle, as well as extra food and clothing.

Other points to remember:
- at any time a walk may become unsafe due to storm damage or the work of bulldozers;
- strenuous walks are unsuitable in high summer, and mountain walks may be unsuitable in wet weather;
- do not overestimate your energy: your speed will be determined by the slowest walker in the group;
- transport at the end of the walk is important;
- proper shoes or boots are a necessity;
- warm clothing is needed in the mountains;
- always take a sunhat; cover arms and legs too!

Goats and shady olive groves — one of the most enduring images of walking on Corfu.

Touring

Most tourists rent some form of transport for part, if not all, of their visit. Car rental is fairly expensive, but the rates become more attractive towards the end of the season (or you can pre-book a car; see page 7). Motorbikes are very good value. **But beware when renting**: many of the cars, to say nothing of the motorbikes, are not serviced regularly; breakdowns are frequent.

Before setting out, check the car (have you got a spare tyre, jack, enough petrol; do the lights work, etc?), and clarify the rental conditions/insurance coverage — in some cases you are not covered for travelling on unsurfaced roads. Don't take a car if you're not happy with it. Usually the internationally known companies are a safe bet, but more expensive. Always carry the agency's phone numbers (and after-hours numbers) with you.

During the high season, youngsters pour onto Corfu. All rent mopeds and motorbikes, many for the first time. The accident rate is appallingly high. Drive slowly and attentively. Also, in the countryside, beware of pedestrians and animals — roads are footpaths to them.

The touring notes are brief: they include little history

The beautiful setting of the Paleokastritsa Monastery, the jewel of Liapades Bay, is best seen from the viewpoint just beyond Lakones (Car tour 3). The same view is enjoyed on foot, from the slopes of Mt Arakli (Walk 12, Picnic 12).

or information about the towns — all this will be in your standard guide book (or freely available from the tourist offices). Instead, I've concentrated on the 'logistics' of touring: times and distances, road conditions, and seeing parts of the island that most tourists miss. Most of all, I emphasise possibilities for **walking** (if you team up with walkers you may lower your car hire costs) and **picknicking** (the symbol *P* is used to alert you to a picnic spot; see pages 10-16). While some of the picnic suggestions may not be suitable during a long car tour, you may see a landscape that you would like to explore at leisure another day.

The large touring map is designed to be held out opposite the touring notes and contains all the information you will need outside Corfu Town. (Note, too, that much of the island has been mapped for the walks: you may wish to refer to some of these large-scale maps from time to time while touring.)

The tours have been written up with Corfu Town (plan pages 8-9) as departure/return point: most of the major resorts are within easy reach of the capital. **Tours 1 and 3 should be given preference if time is limited.** The touring notes *include* time for visits. **Symbols** in the text correspond to those on the touring map; see the key.

All motorists should read the Country code on page 17 and go quietly in the countryside. *Kalo taxidi!*

1 CORFU'S RIVIERA AND PANTOKRATOR

Corfu • Nissaki • Kassiopi • Ano Perithia • Acharavi •
Episkepsis • Mt Pantokrator • Spartilas • Corfu

124km/77mi; about 5-6 hours; Exit A from Corfu Town (plan pages 8-9)
On route: Picnics (see pages 10-16): 1-7; Walks 1-7, 9
*Road surfaces are variable, and most of the driving is on a narrow
winding road. Heavy traffic on the coastal route in peak season. A
motorway was under construction between Corfu Town and Kontokali at time of writing; this may be extended to Dasia.*

Opening hours

Ag Merkourios Chapel (Ag Markos): make arrangements at the
archaeological museum in Corfu Town.

Danilia Folklore Village (near Gouvia): 10.00-13.00, 18.00-22.00
daily except Sundays

This drive is the most rewarding on the island.
Circling the sprawling rocky mass of Pantokrator,
you pass Corfu's Riviera — an unrivalled stretch of
coastline etched with idyllic coves. Olive groves,
splashed with cypress trees, forest the cascading hills
Ascending to Pantokrator, the landscape becomes
harsher. You climb into scrubby hills laced with rocky
outcrops. A plateau, strewn with mounds of rock (see
photograph page 70), leads you to the tiny mountain
peak, from where you can see every corner of the
island and over to the tantalising mountains of Albania
Heading home under a mellow sun, you coil your way
down to Ipsos Bay and a picture-postcard seascape.

Setting out from Corfu Town (Exit A), stay on the
seafront, passing the old and new ports. When you
reach the main north road at a T-junction (🚰), keep
right. The first 16km of this tour follows Corfu's tourist
'tip' — a haphazardly-built-up stretch of unexciting
coastline. But the bold presence of Pantokrator and the
pretty offshore islands of Lazaretto and Vidos are some
compensation.

Kontokali (6.5km 🏔🏔🛖✕🚰△) is the first of the tourist
villages; fortunately, the main road bypasses all of these
resorts. The road to the Danilia folklore village★ forks
left opposite Filipa's Taverna (7km; starting point for
Walk 15), just inside **Gouvia** (🏔🏔🛖✕🚰△). Those
interested in Corfu's history may like to see the remains
of the Venetian naval arsenal near the marina. At the
TSAVROS JUNCTION (9.5km 🏔🏔🛖✕🚰) turn right; soon the
floating chapel of Papandis★ is seen. Bypassing the
resort of **Dasia** (12.5km 🏔🏔🛖△✕🚰), you soon reach the
largest of the holiday villages, **Pyrgi/Ipsos** (15km 🏔🏔
△✕🚰); it stretches out for a kilometre, beside a narrow

Moni Pantokrator, also visited on Walk 7

pebble beach. Walk 9 can end at Pyrgi, the northern end of the resort.*

Continuing towards Nissaki, there are exceptionally good views back over Corfu Town. The road descends to **Barbati** (19.5km ▲▲▲✕), and you catch a quick glimpse of its pretty pebbly beach, set at the foot of olive groves. **Nissaki** (23km ▲▲▲✕❑) is the starting point for Walks 3-6 and a good base for exploring the mountains and coast. Two superb picnic spots are in the neighbourhood (**P**3, **P**4a; photographs on pages 58-59, 60 and the cover).

Winding in and out of the folds in the mountainside, the obvious signs of tourism begin to dwindle, and small, handsome white villages speckle the ridgetops (▲ at Kendroma). Pull over at the KOULOURA/KALAMI JUNC-TION (30km 📷) and survey the scene. Below is Kalami (▲✕**P**4b), still exuding some of the charm so clearly conveyed in Lawrence Durrell's book, *Prospero's Cell.* Kouloura (✕**P**4c), on the northern side of the point, also deserves its picture-postcard rating. A few palms are dotted amongst the cypresses, olives and eucalyptus trees around the shoreline. A small jetty with just a scattering of fishing boats enhances the setting, which is better appreciated from a viewpoint (📷) 500m further along the road. Across the channel lies Albania and its majestic peaks.

Just outside Pyrgi a road strikes left (off the first sharp bend) to Ag Markos (♗✕), a detour of 4km return. Icon and fresco enthusiasts will find two churches of interest here: Pantokrator, which boasts the best-preserved frescoes on the island, and the nearby Byzantine chapel of Ag Merkourios★. Enquire at the local *cafeneion* to visit the former; to see to the latter you must make arrangements beforehand at the Archaeological Museum in Corfu Town.

Climbing again, the countryside opens out. Another enticing cove, splendidly naked of buildings, reveals itself far below the road. A collar of turquoise sea edges the shoreline. If you haven't been down to the sea yet, a detour (7km return) to Ag Stefanos (▲▲▲✕) may be just what you're waiting for. The signposted turn-off lies 3km beyond the Kouloura/Kalami junction. Keep left immediately after you turn off. Admittedly, tourism has already nibbled into this pretty sheltered cove, but it still retains a rustic charm.

The main tour continues towards Kassiopi. You begin to marvel at the wealth of trees in the landscape. In spring the floral splendour of the Judas tree, with its pink and purple clusters of flowers hanging from leafless branches, steals the show. **Kassiopi** (37km ✝▮▲▲▲ ✕🚲△) is my favourite amongst the resorts. With its fishing-village flavour, it verges on recommendable. Walk 4 ends here. The remains of an Angevin fortress crown the scrub-covered headland behind the village. Many of the original walls and towers still stand impressively intact after some seven centuries. And it's worth stretching your legs on the unspoilt headland, where footpaths through the scrub lead to dazzling limestone ledges and tiny shingle coves. In autumn the ground is sprinkled with cyclamen, daisies and dandelions. Needless to say, there's excellent bathing here — head left on foot when you reach the port. In the Middle Ages, Kassiopi's church was the island's most venerated place of worship; it stands on the site of the Temple of Jupiter. Just around the corner from Kassiopi is the pretty seaside village of **Imerolia** (38km ▲✕*P*2). Walk 2 begins and ends here, climbing to the setting shown opposite.

Your next turn-off comes up some 6.5km beyond Kassiopi. Following signs for Loutses, turn left into **Nea Perithia** (▲✕🚲). In the village, keep left and uphill. Looping your way through terraced hillsides, you briefly pass through olive groves. The islands of Othoni (the largest) and Erikoussa (the closest) come into sight, followed by the Antiniotissa Lagoon, nestled in a bed of reeds on a tongue of flat land below. The mountains of Albania, a long line of peaks, trail off into the horizon. On reaching **Loutses** (▲✕), the landscape becomes noticeably rockier. The village trickles down a ridge. Oaks and turpentine trees begin appearing. Beyond Loutses, the untamed countryside shown on pages 62-63 envelops you: craggy, grassy slopes are littered with oaks, wild pears and holly oaks. **Ano Perithia** (51.5km ✗*P*5) hides deep in the folds of Mt Pantokrator. Nestling within the surrounding hills, this almost-deserted village (photographs pages 64 and 74) is one of the prettiest spots on the island. According to the locals, this intriguing village was abandoned some 30 years ago. But as recently as 50 years ago, it boasted a population of 3000, and *nine* churches! It's well worth exploring; Walks 5 and 7 pass through here.

Kassiopi, from the hillside below Bodholakos (Walk 2)

Attractive houses are a strong feature of Corfu's landscape; this photograph was taken on Walk 19, at Ag Mattheos.

Back on the main road, some 300m further on turn off right to the **Antiniotissa Lagoon** and **Ag Spiridon** (61km 🏨🏠✗ℙ1), an intimate cove with a shallow limpid sea, where I highly recommend you stretch your legs on Walk 1. Heading back to the main road, take the first road off to the right.

Continuing west, you head along a sea-flat, where almond groves compete with the olives. The short stretch of pastureland is quickly interrupted by signs of development (🏨🏠✗🖼 at Almiros). In **Acharavi** (67km 🏨🏠✗🖼) *attention is needed* to find your turn-off inland towards Ag Pandelimonas. Although signposted, the road is completely concealed: it's immediately after the Greek Taverna, which is on your right. Ignore the road off left 700m uphill. Cutting inland, you climb into the interior, hugging ridges and skirting valleys, always in the shadow of Pantokrator. Garden plots spill out across the floors of valleys. Dark blades of cypress trees cut through the olive-green countryside. The drawn-out village of **Ag Pandelimonas** (69.5km) passes almost unnoticed. At the junction just outside the village, continue straight ahead. Episkepsis appears, strung out on the ridge opposite. Entering **Episkepsis** (71.5km ✗), keep to the middle (widest) of the three roads ahead. Walk 6 visits this charming village, full of colourful corners. A noticeable Venetian manor sits on the left in the village centre.

The route continues via **Sgourades** (76km), where comfortable old homes lean up against each other. Goats and sheep may cross the road. Some 1.5km pas the village, fork left for Pantokrator (signposted for Petalia/Lafki). The ascent proper begins, and there are fine views across the northwest of the island. Twisting deeper into the bulwark of rock, you come upon a basin of vineyards and garden plots. Rounding a corner, **Strinilas** (82km ✕*P*6) appears, set in hillside boulders and foliage. An enormous elm shades the square. The local wine here is medium-sweet and considered by many Corfiots to be the best on the island. Ask for a *'dopio'*, if you want to try it.

Beyond Strinilas, you cross a ridge and lonely Petalia comes into view, set back in a bare stepped basin. Just over the ridge, watch for the easily-overlooked sign indicating your turn-off (right) for Pantokrator. Less than 1km uphill, pull over for a fine view over Petalia and the northern escarpment (📷). Mounting the plateau, you curl around rocky, scrub-covered hillocks. The landscape becomes more stark. In spring the stones and rocks are covered in flowers; just a short stroll away from the car you can find asphodels, saxifrage, marigolds, irises, fritillaries, veronicas, borage, and several varieties of wild orchids, tiny and ornate, often with the most amazing markings. Please don't pick the flowers! The panorama from the summit of **Mt Pantokrator** (88.5km ✝📷) is unsurpassed on the island. On really clear days, the toe of Italy in the north and the islands of Paxos and Antipaxos in the south can be seen — but during the hazy summer months only the whole of Corfu and the spellbinding sight of nearby Albania can be guaranteed. Ano Perithia stands out like a garden in this bleak landscape.

When you are saturated with views, return to the SGOURADES/SPARTILAS JUNCTION below Strinilas (100km), where you first turned off for Pantokrator, and turn left. Heading south, you're confronted with a splendid coastal view, taking in the bays of Ipsos, Dafnila, Gouvia, and finally Potamos Bay, stretching all the way to Corfu Town. In autumn the surrounding hillsides are soaked in pink heather. Walk 7 begins at **Spartilas** (101.5km ▲✕📷*P*7), magnificently sited on the upper inclines of Pantokrator. No other village on Corfu commands such a view. From here an almost endless series of S-bends drops you down to the Nissaki road (108.5km 🚍). Turn right, back to **Corfu Town** (124km).

2 QUIET CORNERS OF THE NORTHEAST

Corfu • Troumpeta • Valanion • Nimfes • (Roda) •
Sidari • (Perouladies) • Ag Stefanos • Arilas • Afionas
• Arkadades • Ag Georgios • Troumpeta • Corfu

108km/67mi; about 6 hours; Exit A from Corfu Town (plan pages 8-9)

On route: Picnics (see pages 10-16) 8, 9, 11; Walks 8-11

*Roads are generally good, but the country roads are narrow and
sometimes bumpy. Watch out for livestock and pedestrians.*

Once over the escarpment wall, you trail along ridges
and dip in and out of lush valleys. An array of
villages little changed over the centuries lies scattered
across the countryside. The beautiful bays along the
west coast provide good swimming spots — especially
Ag Georgiou Bay, one of the most scenic on Corfu. If
your return coincides with sunset and you can summon
up enough energy for a 15-minute climb, use the notes
for Picnic 9 to catch the island in one of its mellower
moods: from the escarpment wall above Troumpeta,
where no one colour dominates the landscape, the
countryside takes on all the hues of the dying sun.

Follow Car tour 1 to the Tsavros junction (9.5km
⛰▲✕☕), then head left towards Paleokastritsa, passing through **Sgombou** (▲✕; Walks 13 and 14). Leaving
a pretty valley of cypress trees, turn right for Sidari and
Roda (14km; signposted). Climbing through trees
(17.5km ☕), come into **Skripero** (18.5km). Notice the
stately villas on the left, some with arcades. At **Troumpeta Pass** (23km ✕☕🚗P9), where Walk 9 begins, your
views sweep out over the central lowlands of the north.
And behind you, the Ropa Plain, the vast lake of pastureland shown on pages 32-33, comes out of hiding.

Descending into the north, the hills and valleys
become more accentuated. Offshore lie the sharp-
edged Theapondinisi Islands. Take the first turning right
beyond the pass (making for Roda); then, less than 2km
along, turn sharp right again, for Valanion. This narrow
country road twists down into a luxuriant valley full of
trees and gardens. Not far beyond an abandoned,
enclosed hermitage, you enter **Valanion** (29km). Squeezing through this rustic village, keep right out of the
square, towards Roda (indicated by a tiny sign). The
road curls downhill into a wide, open valley, and
crosses another stream. At the first junction you come
to, bear right and head uphill through **Kiprianades**
(31.5km). An eye-catching church, with a verandah, sits
on the left a minute past this hamlet. A left turn at the

next junction quickly brings you down to the main road, where you keep right towards Roda. Half a kilometre along, just past a restaurant, fork right to **Nimfes** (36km ✕*P*8; Walk 8), where a short stroll leads to the delightful chapel shown on page 77.

Returning to the main Roda road, head right. But unless you want a closer look at this unimpressive resort (⌂⌂▲△✕🍴⊕), turn left at the RODA JUNCTION (42km). The road bypasses Karoussades (46km ▲✕🍴⊕), the largest village in the north. At a junction some 5km further on (🍴) turn right to **Sidari** (51km ⌂⌂▲✕🍴), a sprawling resort on a long, but unremarkable sandy beach. Caiques sail to the Theapondinisi Islands from the jetty here (it's often a rough trip!). Half a kilometre along the shoreline, take the first turning right *(not signposted)* to the **Canal d'Amour**★ (⌂⌂▲✕). At a T-

One of the coves at the Canal d'Amour

Coastline at Cape Arilla

junction just over the tidal stream, keep right, and park at the side of the road (in high season it will be very difficult to find a space). This beautifully-eroded clay and marl shoreline, etched with coves, is a superb swimming spot. The bare layered walls, fringed with heather and broom, stand out sharply against the turquoise sea. Local tradition has it that any girl who swims through the channel here — a short stretch of sea passage — while it's in shade, will win the man of her dreams. But tourism has long since taken its toll on this beauty spot.

Return to the main road and head west towards Avliotes. From the PEROULADES JUNCTION (✕) you could make a 5km return detour (not in the main tour) to an impressive beach. To reach it, head through Peroulades (▲✕) and follow the signs for 'Sunset Cafe'. Sunset Beach (▲✕) is a narrow ribbon of sand at the foot of towering white bluffs. On your return through Peroulades, why not stretch your legs with a 15-20 minute walk to the viewpoint shown in the photograph on page 84? Park below the village square (leave plenty of room for the bus to turn round). Then use the notes on page 82 to start Walk 10 on Cape Drastis.

The main tour continues straight to **Avliotes** (58km ▲✕), an unremarkable farming settlement, approached via a low valley embroidered in green squares. Judas trees line the side of the road. At the end of Avliotes, fork left for Ag Stefanos. Haphazard development has scarred the countryside's beautiful rolling green hills around here. The pleasant sandy beach at **Ag Stefanos** (62.5km ▲▲ ▲ ✕), with its backdrop of cliffs, is best seen from the chapel. To reach the beach and its restaurants, turn right at the junction. For Arilas, the next stop, keep left. A gentle ascent takes you uphill to a T-junction; turn left. At the ARILAS JUNCTION (64.5km ▲✕▣) head right for the beach at **Arilas** (▲▲ ▲ ✕). Gravia Island, a sharp oblong rock, sits not far offshore. The Cape Arilla promontory rises boldly out of the sea to the left (photograph above).

Continuing on, briefly follow the seashore. A kilometre along, just over a bridge, fork right on a narrow road signposted for Afionas. The bumpy road winds its way up to T-junction, where you keep right for **Afionas** (69.5km ▲✕▣*P*11). Keep in mind when parking that the bus turns round in the village square, so park *at least* 100m below the square, off the side of the road. Don't miss the unsurpassed views from the top of the ridge behind this village (*P*11; photograph pages 10-11). Short Walk 11 (page 86) is an excellent introduction to Ag Georgiou Bay, a seascape of striking natural beauty.

Heading back out of Afionas, take the first right turn (a *sharp* right, signposted for Afionas Beach). The road is steep and winding. **Afionas Beach** (71.5km ▲✕) occupies the northern corner of the bay, which shows few signs of development. Continuing along the road, midway along the bay you climb above a cluster of beach-front houses. On reaching the crest of a hill, turn down to the right. The road briefly swings inland to skirt a swamp, before reaching the nucleus of **Ag Georgios** (73.5km ▲▲▲✕). Walk 12 visits the southern end of the bay. About 1km along the beach-front, the way veers sharply back to the left and you head inland through a landscape of low-slung hills and valleys. Cypress trees make their mark on the countryside. Keep right at the junction, where a road goes left to Dafni.

Ascending into the pretty hillside village of **Pagi** (78km ▣), keep up to the right and, at the T-junction that immediately follows, turn left to pass through the village. Shortly another road joins from the right; continue along to the left, winding through olive-clad hills. The narrow country roads here are all being widened, so you may well encounter roadworks. At the junction midway through **Arkadades** (83km), turn sharp right. Some 1.5km further on, just past **Kastellani** (▣), you rejoin the SIDARI/CORFU ROAD, where you ascend to the right, to **Troumpeta Pass**. From here return along your outward route. Go left at the PALEOKASTRITSA JUNCTION, then keep straight ahead at the TSAVROS JUNCTION (98.5km), returning to **Corfu Town** in 108km.

3 CENTRAL CORFU'S VARIED LANDSCAPES

Corfu • Paleokastritsa • Lakones • Angelokastro •
Makarades • Troumpeta • Ropa Plain • Mirtiotissa
Beach • (Glyfada Beach) • Pelekas • Sinarades • Ag
Gordis Beach • Kato Garouna • (Ano Garouna) •
Achilleion Palace • Corfu

114km/71mi; about 6 hours; Exit A from Corfu Town (plan pages 8-9)

On route: Picnics (see pages 10-16) 9, 12a-c, 13, 15; Walks 9, 12-15

*Roads are generally good, but narrow and winding. The road to
Lakones is a series of hairpin bends and might prove unnerving for
inexperienced drivers.*

Opening hours

Paleokastritsa Monastery: 07.00-13.00, 15.00-20.00 (1.4-31.10);
persons wearing bathing suits are not permitted entry.

Achilleion Palace: 09:00-16.00 daily

This is a tour that you can do at a leisurely pace,
taking time out for some leg-stretching short walks,
perhaps to some of the suggested picnic spots and then
just a bit further... If you are more fond of walking than
driving, break the tour into a two-day circuit and spice
it up with the many possible short walks. You could
climb the flanks of Mt Arakli, to one of the finest views
in Europe, or check out the breathtaking perch of
Angelokastro and the scant remains of its Byzantine
fortress (Walk 12); stroll across the shepherds' pastures
by Gavrolimni Pond (Walk 14); scale the scrubby peak
of Ag Deka to the hidden monastery of the same name
(Walk 16); wander down to the beach Lawrence
Durrell thought the most beautiful in the world — Mirtiotissa (Walk 15). All these exhilarating and seldom-
visited spots are accessible to everyone; for the most
part, they are only a short distance on foot.

Follow Car tour 2 for 14km, where Car tour 2 turns
right towards Sidari. Here continue straight ahead to
Paleokastritsa★ (25km ⌖▲▲▲△✕⊕▨), a top priority
on every tourist's agenda. It's *the* resort on Corfu, and
with this comes all the benefits and disadvantages of
such a centre. At the foot of the Arakli Hills, on the edge
of tumbling olive groves, rest six enticing turquoise
coves, scooped out of the rocky shoreline. Tourism may
have taken its toll, but no one can deny that the setting,
shown on pages 18-19, is stupendous. Walks 12 and 13
set out from here.

Following the road straight through the village, you
come to the sheer-sided wooded promontory crowned
by the monastery. (Traffic lights have been introduced

The courtyard at Paleokastritsa Monastery

at the foot of the monastery drive, which may involve a five minute wait.) The blindingly-white building dates from the 18th and 19th centuries; however, the monastery was founded in 1228. The pleasant cloister garden shown above lies inside the gates. You may find the collection of 17th- and 18th-century icons in the one-room museum of interest. The monks here don't hide their weariness of tourists. Entrance is free, but one is expected to put something into the offerings box — they may even remind you to do so, should you forget.

Leaving the monastery, you have an excellent view of Lakones (your next stop), strung out along a shelf in the escarpment wall over to the left. Retracing the route for some 3.5km, take the first road off left, signposted to Lakones. The steep climb up a series of S-bends affords superb views all the way. Olive trees arch over the road like large umbrellas; dark pockets of cypresses lie amidst them. Neat rock walls terrace the inclines. Approaching **Lakones** (33km ♠✕*P*12a), the coves below unravel, and soon the view encompasses Liapades and the coastal hills. One kilometre beyond the village, a balcony viewpoint (☜; with limited parking) provides the best spot to take in this magnificent panorama. From here the scars of tourism become minor flaws.

From the viewpoint take the first turn-off left, signposted to **Krini** (36km ♠✕). Remain on this road until it ends at the foot of **Angelokastro★** (37km ■☜ *P*12b). Little remains of the castle, but the 325m/1000ft drops down to the sea from its perch are quite impressive! This Byzantine fortress is thought to have been built around the 12th century by Michael Angelos I. Corfu Town can be seen from the top; hence it was a good place from which to signal the approach of enemy vessels.

Return to the junction just outside Krini and turn left. After 300m turn left again. Park in front of the school just after turning off, then walk along the track for about 15 minutes (or, if you're in a 4WD vehicle, just continue straight on to the end of the track; see the map on pages 86-87. I think this view (📷) — over Ag Georgiou Bay — is every bit as fine as the outlook from the viewpoint past Lakones.

Continuing uphill past the edge of **Makarades** (⌂✖), wind your way up to **Vistonas** (40.5km ✖), where Walk 11 starts, and then slowly mount the escarpment, snatching a view back down over Krini, Makarades and Angelokastro. Pink heather (in autumn) and yellow broom (in spring) bring life to these harsh hillsides in their respective seasons. From the crest a panorama unfolds overlooking both the north and the south of the island. Pull over anywhere along here and take it all in.

Remain along the crest of the escarpment all the way to **Troumpeta Pass** (48km ✖📷**P**9; Walk 9), then head right. Descending from the junction, you look out over central Corfu, rippled with wooded hills. Doukades, the next port of call, is the village snuggled up against the escarpment wall on the right. Some 3.5km down from Troumpeta, turn off right (*attention*: this *sharp* right turn is *not* signposted). The closely-knit hillside village of **Doukades** (54.5km ⌂✖**P**14; Walk 14) has some fine homes in its midst. Leaving the village, ignore a road to the right and another to the left; keep straight downhill. On reaching the Paleokastritsa road (🍴), fork left. Some 800m along, on a bend, turn off *sharp* right towards Liapades. At the junction just below Liapades (⌂✖🍴; Walk 13), turn left, coming onto the edge of the **Ropa Plain**. Heading along through farm plots and vineyards, you're soon passing unfenced pastureland squared off by ditches. Some 5.5km along the Ropa Valley road, you pass the turn-off for Gavrolimni Pond (**P**13), signalled by a sign on the left with a grasshopper on it.

At the Gianades/Marmaro junction, 2km further on, swing right and cut across the plain. Soon come to a three-way junction and head left. At the next junction, turn left again to **Vatos** (70km ⌂△✖🍴⚓). Some 400m beyond Vatos, you round a bend and come to the Glyfada/Pelekas junction, where you continue to the right. The

Ropa Plain (Walks 13 and 15)

dark, wooded slopes of Ag Georgios loom above. This area is the setting for Walk 15, which crosses the island from west to east.

Mirtiotissa Beach, which still remains untouched by tourism, is worth seeing. The turn-off is 2.5km beyond Vatos *and is easily missed,* so watch for a small sign on the right, where a rough dusty track heads off into an olive grove. Park about 0.5km downhill, in a hollow off the track (which is far too steep and rutted for cars). Then slide down to the beach on foot (10min). Legal or not, **Mirtiotissa** (✝✕*P*15; photograph pages 106-107) is Corfu's only naturist beach, where the locals do their bird-watching. Five minutes past the beach the secluded Monastery of Mirtiotissa (Our Lady of the Myrtles) nestles amidst olive groves and pines.

From Mirtiotissa, the tour returns to the main road; turn right and then left at the next GLYFADA/PELEKAS JUNCTION. (If you haven't been down to Mirtiotissa, you can turn *right* here to see Glyfada, another beach set at the foot of cliffs. If you *have* been to Mirtiotissa, Glyfada will be a disappointment.) A steady climb through olive groves brings you into **Pelekas** (76.5km ✝🏔▲✕📷). Turn *sharp left* immediately beyond the first church reached on entering the village (not signposted). This goes to a viewpoint called the '**Kaiser's Throne**' (🏔✕📷). In late autumn, the profusion of crocuses covering this peak may momentarily distract

you from the wonderful panorama. You look across to Corfu Town and Pantokrator, down into the Ropa Valley and over towards the small mountains of Garouna and Ag Deka.

Returning to **Pelekas**, continue through the village, keeping left. Then turn right at the first junction. Travelling along a valley floor patched in vineyards, come to a second junction, where you bear right into colourful **Sinarades** (83.5km ▲▲▲✕). This charming village still retains its country character. At the T-junction (☛) outside Sinarades, head right for **Ag Gordis** (87.5km ▲▲▲✕). Its scenic location has made this village a very popular spot, and parking is virtually impossible. To avoid the centre (near the beach), descend past the hillside apartments then, *just as the road flattens out,* turn left for Kato Garouna, winding high up the olive-clad inclines of Mt Garouna.

Everyone bypasses **Kato Garouna** (89.5km ✕), which looks unappealing on approach. But this cheerful little hamlet is bursting with colour and character. It's too small to drive into; park to the right of the junction and walk in. Turning left at the junction, swing back towards Corfu Town, circling the valley. Keep left all the way, ignoring turn-offs to Ano Pavliana and Ag Mattheos. The valley walls become steeper, with terracing chiselled out of the hillsides. At **Ag Theodori** (93.5km ✕), you come to the turn-off right for Ano Garouna (✕☐), where Walk 16 starts (a detour of 3.5km return). Ano Garouna also boasts a lovely view over the valley and a corner of Ag Gordis.

The main tour passes this turn-off and ends on a cultural note. Continue straight through Ag Theodori to the SINARADES/CORFU ROAD and keep right. At the GASTOURI JUNCTION, 3km along, turn right uphill and pass through **Gastouri** (▲▲▲✕). After 2km you reach **Achilleion Palace★** (☐M), a whim of the Empress of Austria. This ostentatious palace (1892) was a retreat from the goings-on of the Hapsburg Court. After her assassination, it remained vacant until Kaiser Wilhelm II bought it, adding a few touches of his own. The expansive terraced garden, with its panoramic views (☐), makes for pleasant strolling.

Continue along this road to the coast, then head left on the main coast road, back to **Corfu Town** (114km).

4 NOOKS AND CRANNIES IN THE SOUTH

Corfu • (Messongi) • Hlomos • Issos Beach • Argirades • Kouspades • Perivolion • Lefkimmi • Kavos • Gardiki Castle • Korission Lagoon • Ag Mattheos • Corfu

133km/82mi; about 7 hours; Exit B from Corfu Town (plan pages 8-9)

On route: Picnics (see pages 10-16) 16, 18a-c, 20 (Picnic 17 is on the alternative inland route); Walks 16-21

The main south road is well-surfaced but busy; the tour also follows some narrow winding roads.

The highlight of the tour is 'Lake' Korission — really a lagoon. It's a unique, untouched spot, offering something for everyone. Birds — of both varieties — for the bird-watchers, flowers (orchids and catchfly) for the botanists, a shallow beach for the sun-seekers ... and, best of all, peace and quiet for everyone. Beyond Argirades there is little of interest for the passing tourist (unless you would like to see the salt pans on Cape Lefkimmi). Kavos is included for the walkers among you: it's a characterless resort, with absolutely nothing to offer, but Short walk 21 is highly recommended.

The tour heads south via the coastal road. If you're already familiar with this route, you may like to try the alternative inland route described below. In either case, leave the town from San Rocco Square/Platia Georgiou Theotoki and Dimoulitsa Street, following signs for the airport/Lefkimmi (Exit B). At the LEFKIMMI JUNCTION (5km)*, turn left. Heading into Perama, you get a glimpse (📷) of the Vlakerena Convent, joined to the shore by a causeway, and Pondikonisi (Mouse Island). This wonderful setting (see title page) represents Corfu on every brochure. But from **Perama** (7km ▲▲▲✕△🚐)

*****Alternative inland route:** Keep straight on at the LEFKIMMI JUNCTION. Five kilometres further on, turn left for Ag Deka (signposted). Snake up the steep slopes of Mt Ag Deka, covered with loose scatterings of cypress trees. The centre of the island quickly unravels as you climb. Corfu Town and the Khalikiopoulos Lagoon lie not far below. Three kilometres uphill, you pass below **Ag Deka**, a cluster of houses stepping the hillside, with a superb outlook over the gulf to Pantokrator and Albania. Further around the now-sheer inclines, Benitses comes into sight below, cushioned between hills, at the water's edge. Epirus, over the channel, is a series of rounded ridges. A visit to both **Stavros** and **Dafnata** (*P*17), charming pristine villages with very old homes, is recommended. Walk 17 visits Dafnata. The turn-off is the first left beyond Ag Deka. Back on the main road, turn left, to cross over the ridge and descend into the Messongi Valley, woven in olive groves and garden plots. Down on the plain, you pass through the small farming settlement of **Strongili**, then rejoin the main touring route at **Ano Messongi**.

35

The monastery of Ag Deka (Walk 16) is near the alternative inland route.

to Benitses the coastline is built-up and unattractive. Colour in the gardens and the profusion of trees do, however, soften the blow.

Past Perama, you're just above the blue-green sea. Soon you pass the **Kaiser's Bridge★** (✕), a fancy marble jetty once joined to the **Achilleion Gardens★** (Car tour 3) by a bridge, of which a segment remains.

Benitses (12km ▲▲▲✕⊕), where Walk 16 ends and Walk 17 begins, rests at the foot of a thickly-wooded hillside. All that remains of this once-quaint fishing village are the few boats moored to the jetty. But behind this 'Coca-Cola resort', there lies a luxuriant wild garden deep in a valley, a mere 20 minutes' walk from here. If you're a walker, try Walk 16; if you're not a walker, take an evening stroll to the waterworks (*P*16; see notes on pages 15-16). Back on the main road, the remains of a 3rd-century Roman villa suggest that Benitses has been a seaside resort for many centuries (there is also a Roman bathhouse in the village). Beyond Benitses, development thins out to an odd hotel here and there. There is a lovely view of the coastline hills trailing off towards the tail of the island just before **Moraitika** (19.5km ▲▲▲✕🍴⊕).

Approaching the MESSONGI JUNCTION (20.5km), you pass through another eyesore of touristic development. Keep right at the junction, heading inland. At the T-junction at **Ano Messongi** (▲✕🍴) turn left, remaining on the main south road. *(This is where the alternative inland route joins from the right.)* Just over the Messongi Bridge, the road to Ag Mattheos turns off right. Keep straight on and leave the tourist belt behind. The road is wider and faster going, as you travel through olive groves, with the occasional vineyard and garden in their midst. From now on the tour turns off this main road at regular intervals.

The first two side-trips branch off opposite each other at **Linia** (✕🍴). First turn off left for Hlomos (signposted); on your return you will make for Issos Beach from the turn-off just opposite. The ascent to Hlomos affords good views over the Korission Lagoon and, 1.5 kilometres uphill, a roadside viewpoint (⌾☐) makes an ideal spot from which to enjoy the view. Entering **Hlomos** (31.5km ✗⌾*P*18a), park in the small parking bay. For superb views walk a further 100m into the village and follow the signs up to the church, which sits on the hillside above the village. A fine panorama awaits you, encompassing the washed-out hills of Epirus, Lefkimmi Bay, and Cape Lefkimmi tapering off into a fine line. Even Paxos seems close by. Hlomos, visited in Walk 18, is not your typical whitewashed picture-postcard village. As you can see in the photograph on page 117, it has a touch of the farmyard about it; it overflows with character. Houses straddle a steep hillside crowded with a maze of alleys. Every house takes advantage of the panoramic views.

Back at the main road, cross over and wind along through olive trees, vineyards and fields to the dunes of **Issos Beach** (37km, *P*20b). Walk 20 visits this clean, wild stretch of seashore, which sweeps away to the right. The dark slopes of Ag Mattheos rise in the background (photograph page 15). You can climb the crusty sand formations rising from the dunes, five minutes' walk away, for uninterrupted views of the Korission Lagoon.

The next turning off the main road is at **Argirades** (41.5km ▲✗🕮). Halfway through the village, turn left, following signs for Vasiliatika/Petreti. Dropping down through olive groves, you cross an intensively-cultivated basin. An abundance of trees — walnut, loquat, Judas, fig — grows amidst the olives. At the PETRETI JUNCTION, 2.5km downhill, head left to **Kouspades** (45km ▲✗). This *is* a whitewashed picture-postcard village. It's bright and spotless, with very old homes in its midst. You can park off the junction, where you enter the village, and wander up to the left.

From Kouspades there are three possible detours to visit pleasant villages or picnic spots (not included in the overall km readings). You could visit Korakades (*P*18b), some 1.5km along to the right — a sleepy little settlement facing abandon. The picnic setting here is a tranquil spot amongst the deserted houses, in the quiet of olive groves. Or there's Boukari (▲✗), a pretty seaside village on a quiet stretch of coastline 1km north of Kouspades. Petreti (▲✗*P*18c), reached by keeping left at the first junction beyond Korakades, has little to offer. But the picnic spot just south of the village is in a pretty cove at the foot of an olive grove.

Getting acquainted with the southern tip of Corfu is best done on foot. The drive beyond Argirades is unexciting, and Kavos would be best avoided. But Short walk 21, which start out from Kavos, is highly recommended for everyone. It goes to an unfrequented corner of the south — see photographs on pages 126 and 127. The touring route is straightforward: follow the main road through **Perivolion** (54.5km ▲✕⬚), where Walks 18 and 20 end. Then turn off (58.5km) to **Lefkimmi** (61km ▲✕⬚⊕), the largest village in the south. This neglected sprawl is really three adjacent villages (Ano Lefkimmi, Lefkimmi and Potami). Although this sprawling farming settlement can be bypassed, it makes an interesting detour (as long as you keep your eyes peeled in the confusing one-way system). Bird-watchers may like to visit the marshes and salt pans on Cape Lefkimmi, near Alikes. After crossing the picturesque Potamos Estuary, continue straight on. (But a left turn immediately over the river would take you alongside the river to a quiet beach less than 2km away.)

Continue through **Kavos** (66km ▲▲▲✕⊕), until you

The Potamos Estuary at Lefkimmi

reach a junction at the end of this resort. A sign for Corfu Town points to the left here. Keep right, immediately crossing a small bridge. About 200m further on, turn right again towards Spartero. (But if you want to try Short walk 21 to the ruins of Moni Panagia, keep *left* here. After 100m turn right on a gravel track and park. Then see notes on page 125.)

Beyond **Spartero** (70km ✕🖼) the tour meanders amongst the hills, passing through small rural settlements: **Dragotina, Neochori, Bastatika** (keep left at the junction), **Paleochori** (keep right at the junction), and **Kritika** (take first fork off right inside the village). You emerge on the CORFU ROAD at a junction (79km 🚌) west of Lefkimmi.

Turning left, return to **Ano Messongi** and, just past the petrol station, turn left towards Ag Mattheos. Some 2.5km along, turn left again to towards the 13th-century Byzantine fortress of Gardiki. At a junction barely 1km along, turn left. Soon an impressive wall and tower gate rise on a mound in front of you. All that remains of **Gardiki Castle** (🏛) is the exterior octagonal wall with its eight towers. Walk 20 and Short walk 20-1 start here. Continue beyond the fortress, then take the first left turn, to **Mesavrisi** (101.5km ▲✕*P*20a) and the **Korission Lagoon** (700m further on a rough dirt road).

Circling the end of this shallow lagoon, you come to the beach. A causeway of grassy dunes separates the lagoon from the sea. The chaste beauty of the lagoon and the surrounding countryside with its reeds, fields and solitary dwellings, is a world apart from the usual olive-clad hills of Corfu. Grey mullet is farmed in the lagoon for its roe, which is made into *taramasalata*. A very rewarding and easy walk (Walk 20) goes along the dunes past the picturesquely-sited fish farm, over the canal linking the lagoon to the sea (photograph page 120), and on to Ag Georgios.

Botanists can while away the hours here, seeking out the loose-flowered orchid, *Silene colorata* (catchfly), sea stock, sea rocket, sea holly and various sea blites, as well *Medicago marina* (sea medick) and *Otanthus maritimas*. Bird life abounds here in winter and spring, but dwindles in summer. In winter you can see mallards and teal, and many waders — shovellers, pintails, wigeon, and dotterels. Even more birds visit in spring: avocets, on rare occasions glossy ibis, long-legged stilts, small waders like the oyster-catcher, stone

Walks 18 and 20: haystacks outside Perivolion

curlew, little egret, grey, purple and squacco herons …
as well as cormorants, gulls and terns — if you're lucky,
a white-winged black tern.

From here return to Gardiki Castle and, just beyond
it, bear left for Proussadi Beach, circling the foot of
Mt Ag Mattheos. This part of the drive is my favourite:
the gentle inclines harbour a vast museum of olive
trees, with magnificent specimens arching out over the
road. Narrow dirt lanes forking off left go to pretty
coves, including **Skidi** and **Proussadi** (▲✕). Keep right
where a road heads left to Paramona (▲▲▲✕).

Squeezing through a passageway in the hills, you
reach the outskirts of **Ag Mattheos** (114.5km ▲✕), a
sprawling hillside village. A road joins from the right. At
the junction that follows, turn left for Corfu Town. But if
you've plenty of time left, I suggest the toughish ascent
of Mt Ag Mattheos (Walk 19). The village centre, where
you can park, is up to the right.

Descend through a landscape of mossy olive groves,
spiced with thickets of cypress. A brief ascent follows,
up a winding road to the hilltop village of **Vouniatades**
(117km), overlooking the Messongi Valley. Dropping
into this broad basin, you meander through groves
patched with bright pink heather in autumn or sweet-
scented myrtle in spring. Hills rise all around you, and
villages peep out of the wooded ridges.

On reaching the KATO GAROUNA JUNCTION (120.5km),
keep right and, at **Ag Theodori** (✕) pick up the notes for
Car tour 3 from the 93.5km-point (page 34), to return to
Corfu Town (136km).

●Walking ─────────

Few tourists realise the scope Corfu offers for walking, but this book has enough walks to keep Insatiable ramblers occupied for a solid month. For beginners, Corfu is an ideal place to start: the scenic rewards and the countryside experiences soon become addictive. If you're not a walker, the friendly, quieter countryside will soon turn you into one. **All walks are graded and all walkers are catered for in this book.** The majority of the walks — at least in their short or alternative versions — are well suited for **beginners and ramblers**. If you want a *very* short walk, you need look no further than the picnic suggestions on pages 10-16. Hardy **hikers** should head for the Pantokrator Hills — they'll test your stamina. Although the majority of the walks are in the north, the book covers a good cross-section of the island.

Guides, waymarking, maps
A few people on the island run guided walks (enquire at the tourist office), but you will not need a **guide** for any of the walks in this book. Most walks are easily followed, many being along country lanes and tracks.

Some **waymarking** has been carried out on the island but, with the exception of Walk 3, *none* of the walks in this book follow waymarked routes. While you may see waymarks on some stretches of other walks I describe, it is *important that you follow the notes in the book.*

Large-scale **maps** of Corfu are not available from any source. Do not try to obtain large-scale maps from the civil authorities on the island; at the very least, you will be viewed with suspicion. The maps in this book were drawn up 'on the terrain' in 1998.

What to take
If you're already on Corfu when you find this book, and you haven't any special equipment such as a rucksack or walking shoes with ankle support, you can still do some of the walks — or you can buy some equipment at one of the sports shops in Corfu Town. For each walk in the book the *minimum* year-round equipment is listed. Where walking boots are required there is, unfortunately, no substitute: you will need to

rely on the grip and ankle support they provide, as well as their waterproof qualities. All other walks should be made with stout shoes, preferably with thick rubber soles, to grip on wet or slippery surfaces. You may find the following checklist useful:

walking boots (which must be broken-in and comfortable	up-to-date transport timetable spare bootlaces
waterproof rain gear (outside summer months	plastic bottle with plenty of drinking water
long-sleeved shirt (sun protection)	long trousers, tight at the ankles (sun and tick protection)
bandages and band-aids	insect repellent, antiseptic cream
plastic plates, cups etc	knives and openers
anorak (zip opening)	2 lightweight cardigans
sunglasses, sunhat, suncream	plastic groundsheet
extra pair of (long) socks	small rucksack
whistle, torch	

Please bear in mind that I have not done *every* walk in this book under *all* weather conditions. For that reason, I have listed under 'Equipment' all the gear you might need, depending on the season. I rely on your good judgement to modify the list accordingly. Beware of the sun and the effects of dehydration. It's tempting to walk in shorts and to forget that, with the sun behind you, the backs of your legs (and the back of your neck) are getting badly burned. **Always** carry a long-sleeved shirt and long trousers to put on when you've had enough sun, and **always wear a sunhat**. Take your lunch in a shady spot and carry plenty of water and fruit.

Where to stay

If your holiday is going to be a walking one, the most convenient place to stay is Corfu Town. All the buses leave from there. Your next best choice, in terms of public transport *only,* is along the touristy east coast, anywhere between Benitses and Ipsos: Perama, Kanoni, Kontokali, Gouvia. Away from the tourists and the coast, Potamos is another good choice. Staying in Kassiopi, Nissaki, Paleokastritsa, Ag Gordis or Kavos will limit your walking to short walks, especially outside peak season when the bus services are limited.

Renting a car solves the problem of getting to and from areas poorly served by buses. But car hire has its disadvantages: you often have to return to your car on the same route. On some walks, a car can be used in combination with the buses, or you can arrange to be collected by a taxi or friends who will take you back to your car. You could also invest in a moped — they're cheap and will open up the whole island for you, inexpensively! Outside peak season finding a room is no problem (just ask at the local taverna or *cafeneion*), and making overnight stops between walks is great fun.

Weather

The kindest months for walking on Corfu are on either side of summer: April to June and September to October. July and August (with temperatures in the 30°s) are hot and sticky; the only walking you'll enjoy at this time is to and from the beach.

Spring is announced in April with warmth in the sun and an extravaganza of wild flowers, but the rain isn't over yet. By June a rainy day is considered unlucky, and in July and August, a phenomenon. Towards the end of September there's a freshness in the air again, with an occasional passing thunderstorm. In October it's time for a cardigan and, as the month progresses, the cloudy days turn to rainy days. It's not the time for a beach holiday, but the haze-free cerulean sky and lush green fields, with their lavish pockets of autumn flowers, make this an exhilarating time to walk.

In summer the prevailing wind is the *maestros*, a strong nor'westerly which offers slight relief from the relentless hot days and gives cool, more comfortable nights. This gusty wind can last for several days. Another, but less common wind, is the *pounentes* — an ineffectual westerly breeze. A wind that will bother you on rare occasions is the *sirocco* — a hot, sticky, un-comfortable southeasterly that blows for short periods between July and August. It's recognised by its hazy skies. Fortunately this weather is not seen every year.

The prevailing winter wind is the *ostria*, a damp, mild wind from the south. January and February are the coldest months, with temperatures dropping (especially when the *sirocco levante* — SE by E — sweeps in off the snow-clad Epirus Mountains, bringing stormy weather). Ideal winter walking weather is brought by the crisply-cool *levante*, which guarantees clear sunny days.

Outside summer — mid June to mid September — be prepared for all kinds of unpredictable weather! Happy hiking.

Things that bite or sting

In general **dogs** are not a problem. On walks where one does encounter troublesome dogs, I warn you in advance. Pastoral dogs kick up a fuss if you venture too near their flocks/herds, but few are ever more than threatening. If dogs worry you, consider investing in a 'Dog Dazer' — an ultrasonic device which persuades aggressive dogs to back off, without harming them. Write to Sunflower Books for details.

Snakes are a more important problem. Fortunately only a couple are dangerous — the horn viper and the montpellier. The horn viper, easily recognised by its nose-horn and the zigzag or lozenge pattern down its back, is dangerous because it does not move out of your way! All other snakes are as frightened of you as you are of them. The montpellier, a dark grey to black fellow, is much less dangerous. Its fangs are at the rear of its upper jaw and unless it is able to get a good grip on its victim — unlikely when being trodden on — it cannot inject the venom. The biggest snake you'll see is the harmless, phlegmatic four-lined snake, which can reach 250cm/8ft. May and June is when the snakes come out to play ... and September/October to a lesser extent. When walking in long grass, *always wear long trousers, socks, and shoes or boots* — **never** *sandals.* Take a long stick to beat the grass, and be vigilant around springs and water sources in high summer.

Scorpions are nocturnal creatures, and the only time you'll encounter them is when you move logs or rocks. Do so carefully. Their sting is not dangerous, just painful.

Bees and **wasps** abound in summer, particularly around water. Approach all water sources and ponds, etc with care. If you're allergic to stings, make sure you have the necessary pills with you.

Perhaps the biggest nuisance (but only in summer) is the **horse-fly**. Keeping them off you is more exhausting than the walk itself. Long trousers and long-sleeved shirts lessen the problem. Avoid **ticks** by wearing long socks.

You'll also encounter, or hear, lots of **hunters**. They blast away at anything that moves or flies. Don't be afraid to shout and let them know you're around!

The **drinking water** in village fountains is safe but, in outlying areas, **wells have been polluted** by fertilisers.

Greek for walkers

In the major tourist areas you hardly need to know any Greek at all, but once you are out in the country-side a few words of the language will be helpful. Here's one way to ask directions in Greek *and understand the anwers you get!* First memorise the few 'key' and 'secondary' questions given below. Then, always follow your key question with a **second question demanding a yes *(ne)* or no *(ochi)* answer**. Greeks invariably raise their heads to say 'no', which looks to us like the beginning of a 'yes'! By the way, 'ochi' (no) might be pronounced as **o**-hee, **o**-shee or even **oi**-ee.

Following are the two most likely situations in which you may have to use some Greek. The dots (...) show where you will fill in the name of your destination. Ask locally for help with pronunciation; accented syllables are shown in the Index beginning on page 135.

■ Asking the way
The key questions

English	*Approximate Greek pronunciation*
Hello, good day, greetings	**Hair**-i-tay
Please —	**Sas** pa-ra-ka-**loh** —
where is	**pou-ee**-nay
the road that goes to ...?	o **thro**-mo stoh ...?
the footpath that goes to ...?	ee mono-**pati** stoh ...?
the bus stop?	ee **sta**ssis?
Many thanks.	Eff-hah-ree-**stoh** po-li.

Secondary question leading to a yes/no answer

English	*Approximate Greek pronunciation*
Is it here?	**Ee**-nay eth-**o**?
Is it there?	**Ee**-nay eh-**kee**?
Is it straight ahead?	**Ee**-nay kat-eff-**thia**?
Is it behind?	**Ee**-nay **pee**-so?
Is it to the right?	**Ee**-nay thex-**ya**?
Is it to the left?	**Ee**-nay aris-teh-**rah**?
Is it above?	**Ee**-nay eh-**pa**-no?
Is it below?	**Ee**-nay **kah**-to?

■ Asking a taxi driver to take you somewhere and return for you, or asking a taxi driver to collect you somewhere

English	*Approximate Greek pronunciation*
Please —	**Sas** pa-ra-ka-**loh** —
would you take us to ... ?	tha **pah**-reh mas stoh ... ? Come
and pick us up	**El**-la na mas **pah**-reh-teh
at ... (place) at ... (time)	apo ... stees ...

(Instead of memorising the hours of the day, simply point out on your watch the time you wish to be collected.)

Since you may have to rely on taxis for some walks, you might ask your hotel to find a driver who speaks good English. (In the resorts, all taxi drivers speak at least some English.) I'd also recommend you take an inexpensive phrase book. An especially useful book is *Tom Stone's Greek Handbook* — if you can find it on the island. It provides lots of key phrases and pronunciation hints, plus a wealth of practical information.

Organisation of the walks

The 21 main walks in this book are grouped in four general areas: around Mt Pantokrator and the northeast, the northwest, the centre of the island, and the south. You might begin by considering the large fold-out touring map inside the back cover. Here you can see at a glance the overall terrain, the road network, and the orientation of the walking maps in the text. Quickly flipping through the book, you'll find that there's at least one photograph for each walk.

Having selected one or two potential excursions from the map and the photographs, look over the planning information at the beginning of each walk. Here you'll find walking times, grade, equipment, and how to get there/return. If the grade and equipment specifications are beyond your scope, don't despair! *There's almost always a short or alternative version of a walk* and, in most cases, these are less demanding of agility and equipment. If it still looks too strenuous for you, turn to pages 10-16, where the picnic suggestions allow you to savour a walk's special landscape with minimum effort.

The text of each walk begins with an introduction to the overall landscape and then describes the route in detail. The **large-scale maps** (all 1:50,000 and all with north at the top) have been drawn to show current routes and key landmarks. Times are given for reaching certain landmarks. To work out how your walking pace compares with mine, it's a good idea to start out with a couple of the easier walks. This is particularly important if you are relying on public transport at the end of a hike. You'll soon see how your pace compares with mine and make adjustments for your stride ... *and the heat!*

Many of the **symbols** used on the walking maps are self-explanatory, but below is a key.

═══ main road	⛪ church, monastery	⊞ cemetery
─── secondary road	📷 best views	⚡ danger; vertigo
─── minor road	🚌 bus stop	🏵 garden
─── track	🚗 car parking	⚔ military area
---- path or steps	P picnic (see page 10)	⚐ signpost.shrine
⟶3 main walk	⚘ spring, tank, etc	■□ building.shed/corral
⟶3 alternative route	✕ quarry	◼ castle
─── water pipe	⬚ football ground	�📖 page reference

1 AG SPIRIDON • CAPE EKATERINIS • AG SPIRIDON

Distance/time: 4.5km/2.8mi; 1h30min

Grade: easy, but the coastal path is very rocky.

Equipment: boots or stout shoes with good ankle support, sunhat, suncream, sunglasses, swimwear, picnic, water

How to get there and return: 🚌 to/from the beach at Ag Spiridon

Alternative walk: Nea Perithia junction — Ag Spiridon — Cape Ekaterinis — Portes junction: 7km/4.3mi; 2h. Grade and equipment as above; easy descent to begin. 🚌 to the Nea Perithia/Loutses junction (Kassiopi to Sidari bus; journey time 10min). From the bus stop, walk northeast downhill and take the first turn-off to the right; keep straight downhill to the beach, then pick up the main walk below. Follow it to the 45min-point, then use the map below to walk to the bus stop at the Portes junction, 35 minutes along, for a Kassiopi to Roda 🚌.

This short walk is suitable for everyone, from kids to grannies. If you find the rocky coastal path hard going, you can switch to the track a short way inland. Cape Ekaterinis, with its lagoon, tidal streams, and small coves, is very picturesque — and tranquil outside high season. Pines and cypress trees also make a pleasant change from the ubiquitous olive.

The walk starts from the CHURCH at **Ag Spiridon:** continue west behind the main beach. This headland is refreshingly unspoilt, and the shallow sandy beach is ideal for children. The **Antiniotissa Lagoon** lies behind the beach, and you soon cross a small bridge over a tidal stream. This very pretty spot, overlooking the lagoon to the inland hills, is quite untypical of Corfu. Immediately over the bridge, descend to the right, to head along the edge of the estuary. (But if it's high tide,

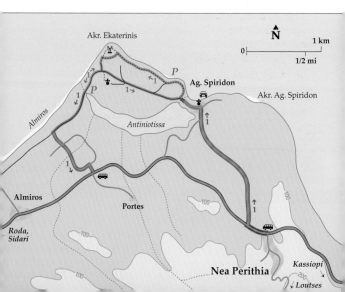

you will have to continue along the gravel road for a few metres, then follow the slightly-overgrown path that strikes off into the scrub, curving slowly to the right to return to the shoreline.)

Once at the water's edge, pick up a path heading round the promontory. A ribbon of pale green water borders the limestone shoreline. Within the first **20min** you're crossing the first cove (Picnic 1). But don't plan to swim here: a bar of rocks cuts across this cove near the shore.

View inland from the second estuary (Picnic 1)

Rejoin the coastal path at the far end of the beach. Quite different from the area not far to the south, this coastline is flat and bare of trees. Inland, the massive mound of Pantokrator bulges out of the landscape. Across the straights, in Albania, the coastal hills climb into mountains. Approaching a BEACON at the tip of **Cape Ekaterinis** (**35min**), the way forks. To continue around the shoreline, keep left, inland from the beacon.

Terebinth trees encroach on the shoreline as you round the headland, and a second cove comes into sight. From here one can see straight along the coast as it curves towards Cape Astrakeri, and Roda doesn't seem very far away. The ruins of an old monastery are visible, in a clump of trees up ahead. A few minutes later you cross the SECOND COVE. Here you pick up a track which takes you to a JUNCTION: turn right. Crossing a small rise, you look down on some sea walls built of rock (probably to protect the estuary ahead); to the right is **Almiros Beach** — an endless stretch of sand. Minutes later come to the second ESTUARY (**45min**), shown opposite, another setting for Picnic 1. This is where the main walk turns back. (*For the Alternative walk, refer to the map to walk on from here to the bus stop at the Portes turn-off, 35 minutes away; the turn-off is slightly to the right of where you meet the main road.*)

The main walk returns from the estuary to the junction, where you keep straight ahead. Barely 100m/yds beyond the junction, you come to a grove of eucalyptus on the right. Take the slightly overgrown path through the grove, to explore the abandoned monastery. But take care around the old walls and the steps: both have crumbled away in places.

Then return to the main track and follow it back to Ag Spiridon, ignoring all side-tracks. Beyond the monastery the way is briefly flanked by tall cypress trees, and avenues of pine lie behind them. It's a cool few minutes. Finally you cross an open, treeless flat area covered in ferns, before reaching **Ag Spiridon** (**1h30min**).

See map on reverse of touring map; see also photograph page 23

Distance/time: 4.25km/2.6mi; 1h40min (add 40min if travelling by bus to/from Kassiopi)

Grade: moderate, with an ascent/descent of 350m/1150ft. A short pathless stretch (10min) over rocky terrain, but not too difficult.

Equipment: walking boots, long socks, sunhat, suncream, long-sleeved shirt, cardigan, raingear, picnic, water

How to get there and return: 🚗 to/from Imerolia (park off the side of the road) or 🚌 to/from Kassiopi. From the bus stop, with your back to the village square, head right to the main road. Turn right on the main road. The walk starts about 15 minutes along, at a path forking off to the left between a bus shelter and the first house on the left as you enter Imerolia.

T his walk is Kassiopi's best kept secret. Not only does it have one of the prettiest footpaths on the island, but in spring it's a garden full of colour. The whole route is drenched with flowers. And not only are there fine views on offer, but a deserted hamlet and a shepherds' outpost are added bonuses. This short hike is best saved for the evening, when it's cooler and the light is at its best. Don't miss it.

The walk starts in the village of **Imerolia**. Head up the valley cutting into the hills that rise up behind the village: the path begins just west of the village bus shelter. A minute along, at a fork, ascend to the left. The path is lined with a profusion of colourful flowers (Picnic 2). The valley floor, crammed with trees, is fresh and verdant; the valley walls lean back steeply on either side. Some **10min** along, ignore a faint fork off to the right; keep left here, to ascend the rocky path up the hillside. Shortly, cross the stream bed and, a minute later, keep right, to begin your ascent into a side-valley. You will remain in the V of this valley almost all the way up to Bodholakos; a steep climb lies ahead. You briefly enter a bosque of kermes oak. Just after leaving this tiny wood, ignore a turn-off to the left, and continue up the zigzag path.

A couple of minutes further along, the path flattens out, and you pass alongside the remains of a STONE PEN on the left. The path forks from time to time, but soon joins up again. Now in the higher reaches of the valley, five minutes from the pen, leave the valley floor and ascend the low crest on the left, ignoring a path to the right (which leads to a well below an walled-in olive grove). Animal paths around here will confuse you but, if you walk in a curving arc to the left, within just one minute you should find yourself to the right of an OLIVE

GROVE set behind stone walls. Remaining alongside the wall, continue up to the right, ignoring all paths forking off right, back towards the walled-in olive grove.

Reaching the end of the wall, you find yourselves below a large farmhouse. This is part of the tiny outpost of **Bodholakos** (**45min**). This hamlet is no longer inhabited, but there are well-tended vegetable plots, and chicken coops adorn the buildings. The old buildings themselves serve as pens for livestock now. Continue up the path, passing to the left of the house. Another homestead, equally as large, appears behind it. And between the two, you'll find a lovely big oak tree to sit under and contemplate your peaceful surroundings and the stupendous view. (But the best viewpoint is five minutes further uphill.)

To continue the walk, stand facing this SECOND HOUSE. There's a chicken pen and a small shed a few metres to the right of it. Between the pen and the shed is a large clump of rock on the hillside ahead. That's your target. Follow the path that ascends to the right of the little shed, keeping straight up and aiming for the right-hand side of the clump of rock. The path then swings left to ascend up over the CLUMP OF ROCK (**50min**). Here's where you can pause for a while and soak up the magnificent panorama that lies before you, with the bare mountains of Albania filling in the backdrop. Just below you can see a corner of Kassiopi; to the right is Avlaki's bay, and behind that the almost-hidden Lake Butrinto in Albania. Sitting here until late evening, under a softening sun, is therapeutic beyond words.

Heading on, the next target is the hamlet visible below, on a crest over to the left (northeast). It will be approached via the right-hand flanks of that crest, although there is no path. To get there, retrace your steps to the top of the OLIVE GROVE below Bodholakos. Follow it downhill for 25m/yds (now with the wall on your right), then fork left on a path. Ignoring any paths descending to the right, head through a gap in a crumbled stone wall, half a minute across the hillside. Continue above the first walled-in olive grove (mentioned earlier in the walk), which is now just below. From here on there is no clear path, and you'll have to do some improvising. Take your time, and watch where you're walking, looking out for both rocks and snakes underfoot.

On the path above Imerolia (Picnic 2)

Just beyond the olive grove, a gap becomes visible in the wall that continues up the hillside. Head through the gap and ascend the flank of the ridge diagonally, pushing your way through tall stalks of sea squill. Approaching the top of the crest, you come upon the remains of another stone wall running down its right-hand side. Keep alongside this wall, but don't cross it. Horses are likely to be tethered to a thick-trunked olive tree not far above the houses, and the horses will appreciate a bit of back-scratching, to give them some relief from the flies.

Continuing down the crest, pass to the right of the buildings and CORRALS (**1h10min**), where the chickens will be running loose. Local shepherds live up here during the grazing months. Make your way over to the fenced-off vegetable garden in the hollow on the left, not far below the houses. Here pick up the path that heads back down to the bay. The path descends alongside the fence, then veers sharply left across the bottom of the enclosure, to continue down the left side of the valley.

Remains of stone walls are a prominent feature in the landscape, and the hillside is a mass of flowers in spring. Over to the right lies the Kassiopi promontory. Descending, you look across to Albania, and Kassiopi slowly comes out of hiding. A good five minutes from the shepherds' quarters, pass through a gate in a fence. Please leave it as you find it. Ignore the path descending to the right here; keep straight ahead. High piles of stones on the hillside, resembling giant cairns, give the impression of passing through an ancient site. Finally, looking straight down into Imerolia's bay (another setting for Picnic 2), descend the right-hand side of the ridge. You briefly enter tall scrub and then emerge on a path alongside houses. The path takes you down to the road at **Imerolia**, just below a SCHOOL (**1h40min**). Your outgoing path is just a short way to the east. Return from here to your car or, if you came by bus, follow the road east, back to Kassiopi (about 20 minutes away).

3 NISSAKI • ROU • PORTA • VIGLA • KOULOURA

See map on reverse of touring map

Distance/time: 8.3km/5.1mi; 3h10min

Grade: fairly strenuous, with a steady ascent of 350m/1150ft lasting 1h15min at the start, and a steep 30-minute descent (slippery when wet) back to sea level at the end.

Equipment: boots or stout shoes with good ankle support/grip, sunhat, sunglasses, suncream, long-sleeved shirt, long trousers, cardigan, raingear, swimwear, picnic, water

How to get there: 🚌 to Nissaki; alight at the Club Med; journey time 45min. Not recommended for motorists, since parking in Nissaki is difficult.
To return: 🚌 from the Kouloura/Kalami junction; journey time 1h

This short walk, well waymarked with yellow dots and arrows, makes an excellent introduction to the island. You climb high above the rocky shores of Nissaki, up through the olive groves and out into the friendly tangle of trees and bushes that patch the rugged countryside. Superb views spill out all around you. Ensconced in these declining hills sits the enchanting hamlet of Rou, in silent abandon, deserted by all but one couple. Coats and trousers hanging on verandahs, doors ajar and windows wide open suggest life within, but not a sound is heard. Descending out of these isolated hills, the enigmatic Albania is tantalizingly close but, alas, its mysteries still lie a mile and a half away, across the straits.

Leave the bus in **Nissaki**, at the CLUB MED GATEWAY (the sign is easily missed, but all the bus conductors know it). **The walk begins** across the road from the gateway; climb the steps at the right of TAVERNA GIORGIO. A minute uphill, just beyond an electricity pylon on the left, the cobbled path rises to the right. Almost at once, head right again, crossing two water pipes. After a few metres/yards, turn left, following the cobbled path uphill, passing very close to the left-hand side of a house.

Some 100m/yds further on, *take care*: turn off on a faint path to the right. The way climbs steadily, and the path becomes more obvious. At a fork a few minutes later, go left, to ascend a path bordered by stone walls. Continue uphill (Picnic 3), ignoring the path to the right a minute further up (by a concrete water tank). The next landmark is a farm building in an olive grove off to the right, with a double electricity pylon nearby: this comes up three minutes later. Be sure to head right at the fork 40m/yds beyond the building and pylon.

On coming to a narrow CONCRETE LANE (**35min**), follow it to the right uphill and come up into the hamlet of **Katavolos**. Continuing up between the houses, you catch views of Albania and Ipsos Bay, with Corfu Town behind it. The best views are still to come. Reaching the last houses, the lane comes to an end. Continue on the track leading off the lane, curving to the right, round the

This was the charming scene which used to greet walkers entering Katavolos. Today these old pillars, no doubt built from the imitation marble quarried nearby, have been replaced by ugly concrete.

hillside. You will remain on this track for the next 40 minutes. Just over 10 minutes along, beyond a faint track forking off to the right, the main track forks: keep left uphill here. The track widens considerably, and you finally have superb unimpeded views across to Albania. Low grey hills roll back to a high escarpment wall of purple. Behind the hills, mirrors of blue betray the inland sea — Lake Butrinto. The only sign of civilisation comes from a patchy green plain back in the hills.

Rounding the hillside, Porta comes into sight, loosely scattered on the ridge opposite. Rou, your immediate destination, soon appears — its tiled rooftops glimpsed through the trees and bushes at the top of the crest not far ahead. You pass a QUARRY (**1h15min**); the imitation marble found here is a much softer stone than marble. Just past the quarry, ascend a track to the left, to enter **Rou**, which lies atop a crest. Just over a hillock, past the first couple of dwellings, the track swings sharply left opposite the only inhabited house*. Continue straight on along a wide grassy path, to come upon the rest of the hamlet, where big open verandahs welcome you. Keep to the path passing in front of the houses. When you reach the last house, ignore the clear path ahead; take the path turning down in an S-bend to the right. You briefly enter a grove of luminous-green trees of Heaven and then emerge on the track again. Turn left along it but, after 25m/yds, pick up the path again, descending to the right.

Hemmed in by thick scrub, the path dips into the gully you've been rounding. Several minutes downhill, you cross a dry stream bed. Less than 10 minutes back uphill (just after crossing a water course), the path fades out. Head straight uphill on a faint trail (don't bear right) and rejoin the path half a minute later. Two minutes later you're in **Porta** (**1h50min**). Two cafés stand on either side of the road where you emerge, but if it's mid-afternoon, the village will be deep in slumber. (Should it be open, try the wine in the first café on your right.)

From here the walk continues to the right. (Walk 5 heads uphill to the left at this point.) Albania sits just in front of you — almost within swimming distance. Around five minutes along, pass a bus shelter on the

*The owners of this house, David and Moira Baker (see acknowledgements), offer refreshments and B&B accommodation, and are happy to see 'Landscapers' on their way.

right. Some 60m/yds beyond it, turn right on the track striking off the bend in the road. Then, just 8m/yds along the track, turn left downhill on a path. The path drops quickly (passing close to a chained-up dog) and emerges on a broad earthen road, which you follow to the left downhill. Barely two minutes down, on a bend to the right, continue straight ahead, rejoining the path on the left.

Coming into **Vigla (2h05min)**, join a concrete drive. Turn left downhill here, almost immediately reaching a T-junction. Keep right, near a *cafeneion*. (Remember these are usually closed between 14.00 and 17.00, so don't rely on them for water.) For the next three minutes follow the road. When you reach the third concrete driveway turning off to the right, follow it downhill. Pass the house, and continue straight down off the drive onto a gravelly earthen path. Remains of the original path momentarily come underfoot. The hillside is very steep; perfect for slipping on! Kalami Bay reappears through the olive trees, luring you down to its green and blue sea. Soon you step your way down onto the driveway of a tourist villa. Turn left here, and then descend a path on the right immediately beyond the swimming pool. Almost at once the path bears left, twisting down through olive trees. A few houses dot the hillside. The path drops down onto a track, which you follow downhill past grassy inclines, overlooking the romantic little cove of Kouloura, neatly tucked into the neck of a headland.

On reaching the ROAD TO KASSIOPI, turn right. At the KOULOURA/KALAMI JUNCTION, keep left. Three minutes along, turn left downhill on a path. It quickly leads to **Kouloura (3h)**. After a rest and perhaps a swim, return the same way to the junction on the MAIN ROAD (**3h 10min**), to catch your bus.

4 NISSAKI • KALAMI • KOULOURA • KERASIA BEACH • AG STEFANOS • AVLAKI BEACH • KASSIOPI

See map on reverse of touring map; see also cover photograph

Distance/time: 14km/8.75mi; 4h20min

Grade: easy as far as Kouloura. Beyond Kouloura there are some awkward stretches, with a possibility of vertigo. The detour to the chapel of Ag Arsenious is steep and rough: care is needed. Height gain no more than 100m/330ft.

Equipment: walking boots or stout shoes with ankle support and good grip, sunhat, sunglasses, suncream, long-sleeved shirt, long trousers, raingear, swimwear, picnic, water

How to get there: 🚌 or 🚐 to Nissaki; alight/park at Bouratika, the last hamlet in Nissaki (bus journey time 45min; ask to alight at the Shell garage at Nissaki)
To return: 🚐 from Kassiopi — back to Corfu Town (journey time 1h) or back to your car at Bouratika (journey time 25min)

Short walk: Nissaki — Kalami — Kouloura: 5.5km/3.5mi; 1h30min. Easy; access and equipment as above, but stout shoes will suffice. *I heartily recommend this for beginners.* Follow the main walk to Kouloura and from there head up to the junction on the main road for your return bus (a Kassiopi bus returning to Corfu Town or Bouratika).

This coastal walk winds its way in and out of Corfu's most beautiful coves. The magnetic charm of these seascapes will not allow you to escape with less than a full day's rambling and swimming.

Leave the bus (or park) at **Bouratika**, the last hamlet in Nissaki. **The walk starts** 100m/yds east of the bus stop, on the corner opposite ANGELO'S SUPERMARKET, by a sign: 'ΠΑΡΑΛΙΑ/beach'. At a junction a minute down, keep left for the beach, as indicated by a sign. Three minutes further on, leave the olive trees and come onto a concrete lane, which takes you down to the first cove, **Kaminaki** — a tourist hamlet with a touch of charm. Your continuation is a path that heads up over the rocks at the end of the beach (to the left). Within the next five minutes, you cross Nissaki Beach (Picnic 4a), passing in front of the NISSAKI BEACH HOTEL. The path continues 50m/yds above its volley ball court, so you have to climb to it through the grounds of the hotel.

Rounding the hillside, and looking across the small cove shown overleaf, you'll see the inconspicuous chapel of **Ag Arsenious** set in rock ahead. Soon after spotting the chapel, fork right down a path to it. This three-minute descent is steep, slightly vertiginous and rocky, but it's a pretty spot (another setting for Picnic 4a). Swimming off the rocks here is great fun.

Continuing along the main path, ignore a fork off to

the left. Keep straight on and come to the next cove, **Agni** (**40min**). A minute along, nearing the end of the beach, pick up the path again, just beyond a concrete driveway. Minutes along, fork right off the main path, to follow the shoreline to yet another (unnamed) beach (Picnic 4b; photograph overleaf). This one is deserted and naked of buildings — quite a surprise since, by late morning (in peak season), the horizon is dotted with boats converging on this cove-indented coastline, like a flotilla of junks seeking shelter from a typhoon.

There is a concrete shed at the point where you first come on to this deserted beach. To continue to the next 'cove of call', Lawrence Durrell's beloved Kalami, head up the dry stream bed at the right of this shed. Half a minute along, bear right, heading between fenced-in plots. Ignore the branch-off to the left a minute along; keep right and straight uphill. Barely a minute up, meet a gravel track and follow it to a concrete lane. Head right on the lane. **Kalami Beach** is just around the bend; unfortunately, an apartment complex now scars this once-idyllic little cove. The lovely large restaurant building you step past (with a terrace bar on one side) was Durrell's home in his *Prospero's Cell* days. Take the steps down to the beach. At the end of the beach, beyond the last taverna, follow a path up to the road.

The main walk now makes for Kouloura, a little over 10 minutes away. (But between the two bays there are some exquisite swimming spots off the limestone shelves. To reach them, turn off the road about seven minutes along: the fairly steep and narrow path turns off immediately past the last house on the right.) Following the road, continue straight on at the junction, ignoring the turn-off to the left. You descend to the idyllic little harbour of **Kouloura** (**1h10min**), in the shade of tall cypresses. Overlooking a small pier sheltering fishing vessels, this is probably one of the most photographed spots on the island. *(From here, those doing the Short walk should return to the junction and ascend to the main road.)*

The next stretch of the walk involves scrambling and a little slipping and sliding; stretches of the path are vertiginous. If this

Looking across to the little chapel of Ag Arsenious

doesn't appeal to you, why not go back to your favourite spot and spend the rest of the day there? Walk back up the road for a minute and then follow the concrete lane off to the right. This takes you to a quiet pebble beach, shaded by tall eucalyptus trees (Picnic 4c). Just beyond the large derelict building at the end of the beach, climb the headland. Rounding a grassy hillside, reach cove number seven — a very small, stony beach tucked into the headland opposite Kouloura. Metres along this beach, climb the hillside to rejoin your path.

About 25 minutes from Kouloura, you cross another beach. This is **Kerasia (1h40min)**, a large and relatively unspoilt cove, again shaded by eucalyptus trees. The only restaurant/bar lies at the end of the beach. (The next section of the walk involves scrambling over rocks and up steep embankments. If you wish to avoid this, or if the sea is rough, just follow the road from this taverna to Ag Stefanos.) Continuing past the bar, on the shore, you're back on a good path. It may be of interest to know that you're crossing the Rothschild property. Don't worry … all beaches in Greece are open to the public. The turret-like construction you'll see is part of the Rothschild villa.

The main path continues down to the beach, but you swing left on a lesser path, to round the point. The next

The unspoilt beach just beyond Agni

cove awaiting you has a fine enclosed orchard sitting off it, but no buildings in sight. Continuing on, follow the shoreline. At times rocks nosing their way out into the sea bar your way: five minutes from the last cove, you have to scramble up a steep nose of rock and slide back down to the shore again. Sorry folks, Mr Rothschild had to make room for his pool here.

Rounding the headland, another cove comes into view. Aim for the centre of it, where a black pipe runs into the sea (it is nothing more sinister than water effluent from the olive press in the village above). Alongside the pipe, the path, which is a little overgrown at the outset, runs inland through a cool glade. Emerge on the road from Kerasia and turn right.

Descending through olive groves, the tenth cove comes into sight. This charming inlet, **Ag Stefanos (2h 50min)** has become another victim of tourism, but still retains a good portion of its original rustic flavour. Leaving it behind, follow the road. Some 25 minutes uphill, not far past a turn-off to a military installation, turn off right on a track. A further 25 minutes brings you down to **Avlaki Beach (3h40min)**, set in an open curving bay cut deeply into the coast.* At the far end of the beach, join the Kassiopi road, and follow this out to the main road, a little over half an hour away. Turn right on the main road and in 10 minutes come into **Kassiopi**, where the bus leaves from the VILLAGE SQUARE (**4h20min**).

*Four minutes from here there is a pleasant little cove, accessible only on foot or by boat. To visit it, turn right towards the headland. A footpath leads up the slope; it soon becomes a tunnel through bushes and takes you above the cove, which is usually deserted.

5 NISSAKI • PORTA • ANO PERITHIA • LAFKI

See map on reverse of touring map; see also photograph page 74
Distance/time: 17km/10.5mi; 6h

Grade: strenuous, with an overall ascent of 600m/1970ft; only recommended for experienced/adventurous walkers. Snakes are not uncommon in this terrain.

Equipment: walking boots, long socks, jacket/cardigan, sunhat, sunglasses, suncream, long-sleeved shirt, long trousers, raingear, picnic, plenty of water

How to get there: 🚌 to Nissaki; alight at the Club Med; journey time 45min. Not recommended for motorists, since parking in Nissaki is difficult.
To return: 🚌 from Lafki (only one departure Mon-Sat at 15:30; recheck this departure time before setting out!)

If you're an experienced walker and don't mind floundering over wild tracts of ground, this is a fantastic hike. You cross the vast flanks of Pantokrator, where the shepherd roams with his flocks and herds of goats ... and occasionally the hunter roams with his gun. Rustic hamlets and villages lie en route; in between, rocky hillsides slide down into sheer, narrow valleys. Following the faintest of paths — and often just your nose, you trail through the loneliest landscape on the island. The countryside is undeveloped (in the best possible sense of the word) and rich in flora. With its striking panoramas, this walk lacks for nothing.

Start out by using notes for Walk 3 (page 53). Follow the route to **Porta** (**1h50min**), where Walk 3 keeps right. Here head up left through the village. Three minutes above the church, come to a junction and turn right on a road. Judas trees lie off the route. In spring their rich pink-to-mauve flowers hang in clusters off their leafless branches — a splendid sight. Tradition has it that this is the tree on which Judas Iscariot hung himself after denouncing Christ and, according to legend, the once-pale flowers turned pink in shame.

Mountainous Albania stretches out before you, and Lake Butrinto is visible, although partially hidden behind the coastal hills. The tiny lighthouse island of Peristator lies off Cape Varvara. Santa is the small village two ridges away. Looking up the road, you spot Mengoulas — your immediate destination. This hamlet perches high on a hillside knoll.

A good 10 minutes along the road turn left up a concrete lane into **Mengoulas**. Barely five minutes up, a Venetian manor greets you (**2h20min**). Take the path up alongside the mansion. A minute up come onto a faint track. Keep left here, then fork right on a path, swinging

On the descent to Ano Perithia (at about 3h35min into the walk, just after crossing the narrow valley).

up behind a house. Continue straight up the crest, passing some CORRALS on the left. Just beyond them, a fence blocks the way. Head through the gate here (leaving it as you find it). Joining a track, turn right along it. From here your target is the oblong stone building just below the top of the crest ahead. One minute along the track, on a bend, follow an animals' path up the face of the hill. The path soon fades out and you improvise your route, climbing steeply over rough terrain. Jerusalem sage covers the inclines. Albania unfolds as you rise. Emerging on the TOP OF THE CREST (**2h50min**), just above the stone building, you enjoy fine views all around. Albania sits in a soft haze, accentuated by a deep blue sea. Porta, buried in the landscape, adorns the crest of a ridge below. Inland, straw-coloured hills, stained with patches of rust-brown fern, flatten out into hilltop plains. Head along the ridge to the right, to a CAIRN, then descend slightly, to take in the lovely view of Kassiopi nestled around a cove.

Before leaving, it's best to locate your ongoing route — a path climbing the flank of the ridge opposite. Keep in mind exactly where it begins. Heading directly down the hillside from the cairn, pick up a path of sorts cutting across in front of you, about two minutes downhill (the path is less visible in spring, when it's camouflaged by high grass). Follow this path to the left. Near the valley floor, the path bears left, rounding the valley. To reach the start of the path identified from the cairn, you have to push our way through Jerusalem sage and then cross some terracing.

Ascending the path, you come up to a lone wild pear tree. From here continue round the hillside, gradually

making your way to the top of the crest, a few minutes
away. From the top of the crest, you'll see a rubbish
dump just below you (the smell alone will lead you to
it...). Climb down to the dump and follow the track
leading out from it. Meet another TRACK (**3h20min**), on a
bend, and follow it to the left uphill, surrounded by
grassy hills. About five minutes up, leave this track.
Attention: locating the turn-off is difficult. Your ongoing
path descends off a slight curve, about 50m/yds below
the point where the track bends *sharply* left. Two wild
pear trees stand by the track at this point. The path
descends below these trees, before heading round the
grassy slope. When the path fades, aim between the
two wild pear trees in the middle distance. You pass
behind a DERELICT STONE BUILDING, slightly off to the right.
Here the path should reappear, and you follow it
downhill along the right-hand wall of the valley, above
terracing. The valley narrows considerably and, 10
minutes off the track, you cross the valley floor and
climb the steep path on the far side. The pleasant sound
of ringing bells alerts you to flocks of sheep, but pin-
pointing them amongst all this rock is another thing!
Wild pears are the only trees hardy enough to survive in
this rocky terrain.

Ano Perithia, from the cobbled path (Picnic 5)

Ano Perithia begins to unravel, building by building. A church belfry appears not far below (so, if you have difficulty following the notes from here because the path has petered out, just make your way towards its belfry). Crossing very rocky terrain, the path forks just as it begins to zigzag down the hillside: the lower path is less overgrown. Closer to the village, the path is very faint. It takes you across a dry stream bed, to a track just above the village (this is the track to Lafki, which you will follow later). Turn left on the track then, just before the church, fork right on another track, to visit the village. When you are opposite the church, fork right on a cobbled path into **Ano Perithia** (**4h20min**; Picnic 5), where you can refuel at either of the restaurants for the final leg of the hike.

After a break, head back to the Lafki track above the church and turn right along it. You will follow this track all the way to Lafki. From the opposite side of the valley, you have an excellent view back over Ano Perithia. Notice the interesting hill formation below the track, resembling a pack of propped-up cards. An hour from Perithia, you round the nose of a ridge and pass above lush pastures. A large abandoned dwelling sits above the track a little further on, and a deserted hamlet hides in the hillside trees above. Soon you're overlooking an impressive valley scarred by a large quarry. Lafki lies on the far side of it. You enjoy a good coastal view of Acharavi not far below, with Roda beyond it. From the quarry, emerge on a road and turn left. In two minutes you're in **Lafki**. The BUS STOP (**6h**) is in the village centre.

6 NISSAKI • PALEO XORIO • (MT PANTOKRATOR) • STRINILAS • EPISKEPSIS • SFAKERA • RODA

See map on reverse of touring map; see also photographs pages 2, 12, 21

Distance/time: 21km/13mi; 6h50min

Grade: Strenuous, with a climb and descent of about 800m/2625ft. Only fit walkers should attempt the entire hike. Most of way the hike follows tracks, but there are two short sections of pathless ascent up rocky slopes.

Equipment: walking boots, sunhat, sunglasses, suncream, long-sleeved shirt, long trousers, cardigan, jacket, raingear, swimwear, picnic, water

How to get there: 🚌 to Nissaki; ask to alight at road to Vinglatsouri; journey time 45min.

To return: 🚌 from Roda (journey time 1h). If you cut short the hike, there are buses from Strinilas (not Sundays/holidays; journey time 1h20min) or Episkepsis (not Sundays/holidays; journey time 1h30min).

Short walks

1 Nissaki — Paleo Xorio — Nissaki: 8.5km/5.3mi; 3h. Grade: a climb and descent of 450m/1475ft, mostly on country lanes and tracks, with a short stretch of path. Accesss and equipment as main walk. Follow the main walk to Paleo Xorio and return the same way.

2 Strinilas — Episkepsis — Roda: 9.5km/6mi; 3h10min. An easy downhill walk on tracks; stout shoes will suffice. Access: 🚌 Lafki bus to Strinilas; return as main walk. Follow the main walk from Strinilas (the 3h50min-point; see page 69).

Alternative walks

1 Nissaki — Paleo Xorio — Ano Perithia — Loutses — Kalamaki Beach: 14km/8.8mi; 5h. Strenuous ascent of 680m/2230ft; only for experienced walkers. Some pathless sections both up and down steep rocky terrain. Equipment and access as main walk; return on 🚌 from Kalamaki Beach to Kassiopi, then change buses for Corfu Town (journey time 1h30min). Follow the main walk to the pass at the 2h20min-point and keep left at the T-junction. At the first bend in the track, just beyond the animal shed/pens below the road, join Walk 7 at the 2h40min-point. Pick up the notes on page 74 to descend to Ano Perithia and continue to Kalamaki Beach.

2 Nissaki — Paleo Xorio — Porta: 11km/6.8mi; 3h50min. Strenuous climb and descent of 680m/2230ft, but mostly along tracks. Short stretches of clambering over rocky terrain. Equipment and access as main walk; return by bus from Porta. Follow the main walk up to the pass (the 2h20min-mark), then keep right. Five minutes later come to a lay-by with a bench, at a junction. Here turn right for Porta. At the next junction, 35 minutes later, head right — but, before you do so, continue on for another minute or so for stunning views over Porta to Albania. Just below the junction, pass a shed and take the fork to the left. Thirty minutes downhill, turn right for Porta, a good five minutes away. Pick up the bus at the turnabout/parking area in the village.

You begin this hike scaling the harsh, rock-smeared slopes of Pantokrator. On route you pass through the ruins of Paleo Xorio — a medieval village normally seen only from the summit of Pantokrator. The verdure that envelopes it betrays its presence in this stark hilly landscape. Every crest you master reveals spectacular views. Atop Pantokrator, before gliding down to the sea, you cross a vast plateau littered with sharp rocky mounds. In springtime this great spillage of rock turns into a rock garden, as myriad flowers appear. Finally, cutting your way down through curving valleys, you make for the sea. A note of cheer returns to the landscape as you weave your way through friendly, shady olive groves and drop into a valley full of trees.

Alight from the bus at the road to Vinglastouri (just two minutes past Glyfa Beach, as the bus enters **Nissaki**). Since the drivers do not know this stop, watch for the Glyfa Taverna on the right, and press the stop button on the next seaward-curving bend. **Begin the walk** by heading up the road opposite the bus stop; it is SIGNPOSTED TO VINGLATSOURI, and there is a bus shelter on the right. The steep climb up this tarred road is mitigated by the wonderful views. With every turn you're overlooking the glorious Kerkyra Gulf, through olive trees. On the left is Albania, on the right, Ipsos Bay. The shimmering sea lies like a plate of glass, with not a ripple to be seen. Soon a shoulder of Pantokrator rises on the far side of a ravine; Barbati Beach lies below.

On coming into the ravine-side hamlet of **Vinglat-souri (40min)**, you encounter a fork: keep left for Paleo Xorio. Five minutes up from the fork, and just after an S-bend, you can take a short-cut on a steep path ascending to the right, through olive groves. Rejoining the lane (which has now reverted to concrete) a few minutes up, leave the olive groves and come onto a hillside fresh with grass. Heavy sprinklings of yellow-blooming broom lie below. Through the sheer ravine walls the coastline unravels. On fine days Corfu Town and the airport lagoon are picture-postcard clear and, beyond, the dark blue tail of the island is visible.

At a T-junction with a track, turn left for Paleo Xorio. A mass of flowers lines this track in springtime. About five minutes uphill, at a fork, leave this main track and turn left down another track, into the valley below. A couple of minutes later, when the track swings left, keep straight ahead on a path (a yellow arrow pointing in the opposite direction marks the spot). On the far hillside, a corral is visible: you will pass to the left of it. At the bottom of the valley, you cross a dry stream bed by an old fig tree and ascend a beautiful old stone-laid path on the far side. At times the path is a bit faint; keep watch for the yellow arrows. You're climbing to the track above, and the path passes below a large wild pear tree which sits just below the track. Beyond the CORRAL, at a fork, keep left.

Meeting the track, head along to the left. Go quietly past the beehives here. The views are superb; the radiant blue gulf, framed by the ravine walls, recaptures your attention. Heading deeper into the valley, you round a bend and see the ruined buildings of an old village up ahead. Fork right on a track just below the

Alternative walk 2: On the descent to Porta, with Albania in the distance

Paleo Xorio

ruins, then follow a path off the end of the track and curve round to the right up through the ruins of **Paleo Xorio** (**1h40min**). You pass the shell of a large old house, with a stone table outside. Where better to take a lunch break? Just a little further along are the old wells, on either side of the path. The water is drinkable, but be extremely careful when drawing it up; the well is very old and the rocks built across the top of it are not secure. (Beware also, during high summer, of hordes of wasps. Draw the water quietly.) This old village is an intriguing place to explore, but do so with the utmost care, as some of the buildings could be in a dangerous state of decay. *(Short walk 1 turns back here.)*

Leaving Paleo Xorio involves a bit of scrambling; there is no path. Bear in mind that you are aiming for the track above the village. Standing between the WELLS, with your back to the village, ascend the hillside on your immediate left — making first for the church on the crest above (and slightly behind you). From the church head up the crest to the track. It's a steady climb up through the remains of terrracing and scrub.

Reaching the track, turn right and follow it for about half an hour, up to a PASS (**2h20min**). If you're not being battered by the winds, plonk yourself down and soak up this magnificent panorama. To the north, down through the V in the hills, an another almost-deserted village is visible — Ano Perithia (Walks 5 and 7), with the mountainous interior of Albania in the background. In summer there's nowhere cooler than this pass!

For the main walk *(and Alternative walk 1)* turn left at the T-junction here. *(But turn right for Alternative walk 2.)* Within 20 minutes you reach the road that climbs to the summit of Pantokrator. If you haven't already seen the monastery (photograph page 21), it's less than 30 minutes uphill (a detour *not* included in the overall times). Continuing to the right, you cross the plateau, weaving your way around crusty mounds of rock. Sunken, grass-lined hollows create green waterless lakes. This is goat country. A little further on, the north coast appears, with a view over Cape Astrakeri. The return to civilisation comes when you catch sight of the small country village of Petalia below the road. Fifty minutes down from the Pantokrator junction, you emerge on another ROAD. Turn left and, five minutes later, enter **Strinilas (3h50min)** — by the pretty village square, shaded by a gargantuan elm tree. If you feel you've done enough today, you can catch a bus here. *(This is where Short walk 2 begins.)*

Just beyond the square, and immediately after the sign denoting the edge of the village, turn right down a concrete lane. At the T-junction 30m/yds ahead, turn left down a track (Picnic 6), which will take you to the doorstep of Episkepsis. On the way you'll spot Ag Triada, the magnificently-sited monastery visited in Walk 8, perched on the highest hill in the north. The route drops down into a concealed combe before crossing a shelf of fallow plots. Winding down through olive groves, come down onto a ROAD **(4h50min)**. Turn left uphill, entering a charming archetypal farming community. Take the first turn-off right down an alley flanked by houses, to pass by the church. Keep downhill and, at the junction, descend another alley to the left, to the main road in the centre of **Episkepsis (5h)**. Notice the charming three-storied Venetian manor on the right here.

Turn left on the main road; you will come to three cafés. (If you're winding up the walk here, the bus stop is 30m/yds beyond these cafés, before the sharp bend.) The final leg of the main hike begins by one of the cafés — the Ellikon. Head down the wide concrete lane just alongside it, passing a church and school within a minute. Continue on through a severed arm of the village, ensconced on a ridge. Beyond the houses, ignore a faint fork to the left. The concrete gives way to a narrow farm track as you descend this ridge, beautifully hooded in olive groves. About 10 minutes from the village, the track forks. Climb up to the left, rounding the nose of a ridge, then drop down into a deep, shady valley on the far side. It's very pretty countryside; the valley floor displaying a rich assortment of foliage.

You cross a small BRIDGE and, gradually, the hills fold back to disclose a boat-shaped valley. Recross the stream several minutes later. A minute after this stream crossing, join a track coming from the right and follow it to the left, heading along the opposite side of the valley. Oaks make a brief appearance, then a pleasant

Descending the flanks of Mt Pantokrator, you cross the plateau, weaving your way around crusty mounds of rock, where sunken grass-lined hollows create green waterless lakes.

grassy patch appears below the track. Leaving these abrupt valleys behind, your way begins opening out. A little over 10 minutes from the last stream crossing, ignore a faint track branching off to the right and, two minutes later, another track forking off right. Wending your way through the valley floor, you reach the coastal plain.

On coming to a T-junction, turn left. In a couple of minutes you reach a road on the outskirts of **Sfakera** (**6h20min**). Turn right and join the main road to Roda. A further 30 minutes along this road brings you to **Roda**'s beach. The BUS STOP (**6h50min**) is just where the road meets the sea — on the left side of the road, north of the crossroads.

7 SPARTILAS • MT PANTOKRATOR • ANO PERITHIA • LOUTSES • KALAMAKI BEACH

See map on reverse of touring map; see also photographs pages 21, 62-63, 64 and opposite

Distance/time: 15.5km/9.6mi; 5h20min

Grade: very strenuous, with an ascent of about 600m/1970ft and descent of 906m/2970ft. For experienced walkers only. Short stretches of path are partially overgrown, and one short stretch is vertiginous. It is very rocky on the top of the plateau — take your time. The descent to Ano Perithia involves improvising your way down a steep rocky slope. Do not attempt in bad weather or when there is low cloud.

Equipment: walking boots, sunhat, sunglasses, suncream, long-sleeved shirt, long trousers, raingear, swimwear, picnic, water, plenty of insect repellent in summer (when there are flies galore)

How to get there: 🚌 to Pyrgi/Ipsos (30min) and taxi from there to the village centre in Spartilas. (There is also a Spartilas bus, but it doesn't give enough time for the walk.)
To return: 🚌 from Kalamaki Beach to Kassiopi; change buses for Corfu; journey time 1h30min.

Short walk: Spartilas — Taxiarkhis Chapel — Spartilas: 3km/1.9mi; 1h30min. Fairly strenuous, with ascents and descents of about 280m/920ft; the path is partially overgrown, and there is one short vertiginous stretch. Equipment as above; access: 🚗 to/from Spartilas (park at the northern end of the village). Follow the main walk up to the chapel and return the same way.

Spend a day on the inhospitable slopes of Pantokrator — clambering up animal paths, pushing your way through scrub and floundering over rocks. No walk on the island offers so much adventure, or discomfort. For those who want the panorama without the hassles, there's a comfortable tarred road to the top. From the summit (906m/2970ft), your views stretch as far south as the islands of Paxos and Antipaxos and — on rare occasions — to the toe of Italy. What one remembers most, however, is the captivating view of neighbouring Albania. Ano Perithia, the most isolated village on Corfu, rests in a hollow of trees not far below you, girded by buffer hills of bright grey rock. This shuttered village, deserted save for two unobtrusive restaurants, alone makes the long, arduous hike worthwhile.

Ask your taxi driver to drop you outside the community office (pronounced 'Kee-**no**-ti-kon gra-**fee**-on') in **Spartilas**. (If you come by bus direct to Spartilas, this office is the second stop in the village, and a sign outside reads: 'ΚΟΙΝΟΤΙΚΟΝ ΓΡΑΦΕΙΟΝ ΣΠΑΡΤΙΛΑ'.) **Start off** by heading up the right-hand alley diagonally across the road from the community office, climbing up between hillside houses. Less than half a minute up, behind the church, the path forks. Take the steps to the left. When you reach a concrete lane at the top of the steps, follow it uphill. It becomes a track. Three minutes up from the road, on a bend, leave the track and continue straight ahead on a path (the first turn-off you reach). At this stage small red dots mark your route.

The first few minutes across these hillside plots require *attention*. Pass above an uninhabited house a minute from the turn-off. When the path forks, keep left (continuing in the same direction). Then ignore a faint turn-off left. Four minutes from the track, the path abruptly swings up to the left between stone walls in varying stages of decay. It then veers back to the right again, gradually ascending above olive groves (Picnic 7) and heading along the foot of the escarpment. This much narrower path, hemmed with vegetation (including scratchy spiny broom), will remain your route all the way to the top of the plateau. There is a short stretch of vertiginous path along here.

Rounding a side-valley, you pass a ROCK (**15min**) jutting out from this scrub-covered slope; from here you have a foretaste of the panorama to come once you've reached the top. Bushes of holm oak, *Pistacia lentiscus*, spiny broom, heather and Jerusalem sage hem you in, and the path is littered with empty shotgun cartridges. Approaching the plateau, the terrain becomes rockier, pushing its way through the mat of vegetation. Clumps of heather, with purple and pink flower-heads, stand out on the hillside. Shiny-leafed strawberry trees begin appearing.

On reaching the PLATEAU (**45min**), don't miss the branch-off to the chapel of **Taxiarkhis**, barely a minute along. The path to it is over to the right and ascends through the remains of terracing. Holm oak bushes conceal the chapel, which stands just at the edge of the plateau. From here there is a spectacular panorama over the sweeping blue bays bitten out of the coastline. Stretching out before you, the island rises into a portly midriff, before tapering off into an undulating tail. And you have a bird's-eye view down onto Spartilas. Perhaps you'll be as dismayed as I was recently, to find the chapel door ajar and the exquisite wall and altar frescoes left to the ravages of nature … and man. Believe it or not, most of them are still well preserved. *(The Short walk turns back here.)*

Before heading on, verify your ongoing route from

behind the chapel. The way is through the very slight, bush-filled valley that heads directly towards Pantokrator (with the very obvious radio mast). Back on the path, keep straight ahead. This stretch of the walk is very well waymarked, perhaps overly so … as you will see later. Thyme and spiny broom layer the gently-subsiding inclines. Five minutes from the chapel, just after climbing the remains of a terraced embankment, the path fades. Keep straight ahead, bearing right towards the valley. A minute later, pass through an intersection, to see a STONE BUILDING (**55min**) just below the path. A path off to the right at the building takes you to a beautiful stone-laid WHEAT THRESHING FLOOR hidden in the trees. It's a very pretty spot. Ignore all the paths striking off uphill and out of the valley. Your way burrows through the scrub lining the V in the slope. At intervals, terraced plots appear through the bushes on the right. In summer this shaded path is a welcome break from the hot sun; in spring moss cushions the surrounding rock.

About 10 minutes from the stone building, you leave the scrub, but continue up the valley floor. When you notice a track above you, scramble over the boulders at the side of the track and climb up to it. On the first bend, when the track swings right, take the well-trodden path up to the left, through terraced fields. Now clamber up and over every stone wall, keeping an eye on the waymarking. Five minutes above the track, you come out onto another, higher level in the plateau. A grass-covered plain leads up to a choppy sea of rocky hummocks rising and falling all round. Beyond this unruliness lies Mt Pantokrator. Follow the waymarking: in summer, within seconds of entering the dry grass, flies will descend on you by the thousands, trying to crawl into every orifice laid open to them. Don't even cough, it's too risky! The bright side of this onslaught is that — tired though you may be — you certainly quicken your pace! (*If at this stage cloud or bad weather threaten, do not attempt to go further!*)

A couple of minutes across this upper plateau, the route veers left, following a slight depression. You briefly leave the grassy plots and head across a rock-strewn plain. Then the way becomes like an obstacle course, as you climb in and out of sunken pastures amidst this mass of rock. *Keep your eye on the waymarking*; it's easy to head off in the wrong direction!

Ano Perithia, with one of its nine churches in the foreground

Ignore all the lettering waymarks; *follow* the arrows and dots. Small, long-stemmed *Euphorbia myrsinites* grows up here amidst the rock, and in autumn golden-headed thistles *(Pallenis spinosa)* cover the rocky slopes. Closer to Pantokrator the mounds become sharper and the hollows deeper.

Crossing a crest, the mountain road comes into sight. From here on the waymarking is faded and infrequent. If you lose the trail, just make for the road. Descending, remains of an old path appear. Dip down into a large valley cutting across in front of you. Bear left along it and, when you reach a double terraced wall, pick up a clear path ascending to the ROAD (**1h45min**).

Turn right, making for the summit and the monastery, passing a pretty shaded hillside hollow. A little further on, you're overlooking Ano Perithia, a haven of greenery, swallowed up by a mass of tumbling, rocky slopes — a welcoming sight in this bleak landscape. Passing under the belfry, you enter the grounds of **Moni Pantokrator** (**2h10min**). The towering radio mast certainly doesn't help this already-naked enclosure. The back of the building, with its cloister arches, is more appealing (photograph page 21). There are some faded 17th-century frescoes in the chapel.

Descend the road from the monastery and take the first track turning off to the right. Follow this track for the next 15 minutes, before beginning your improvised descent to Ano Perithia. On rounding a bend in the track (just before the pass and the turn-off to Paleo Xorio), you look down onto a large shed for livestock just below the track (**2h40min**). The descent begins just before the shed but, for orientation, it's a good idea to walk on to the pass to identify where you are going — Ano Perithia. Then return to the bend in the road and turn off into the valley, just beyond the shed. Keep to the top of the crest for a minute or so, then descend to the right taking care not to go too far down into the V. Rounding the hillside, you're soon overlooking Ano

Perithia. Your target from here is the church immediately below, at the foot of the hill you're rounding.
Twenty minutes down, approaching the church, look
for a gap in the ferns and scrub, which opens your way
to the nearby track. Coming onto the track, head along
to the church (which should be on your left). Fork right
down the track just before the church and then bear
right on a cobbled path to descend into **Ano Perithia**
(**3h20min**).

Leaving Ano Perithia, head up to the right of Taverna
Capricorn, between more empty, shuttered houses.
Tall, yellow-flowering stems of mullein line the roadside. Follow this road all the way to **Loutses** (**4h**), which
appears before a stunning backdrop of glimmering sea
and the enormous shadowy mountains of Albania. (If
you're catching a bus here, ignore the first bus stop
(where the bus turns around); go on to a second bus
stop less than 15 minutes further on, where you can
wait in the comfort of a café.)

Those bound for Kalamaki Beach, however, turn up
the first road branching off right, five minutes below the
first bus stop/turnabout. Pass through a small cluster of
houses, keeping right at the first fork (a minute along),
and left at the second (three minutes later), following
the tarmac road. At the end of the road lies the tiny
village of **Anapaftiria** (**4h20min**). From here follow the
wide farm track that continues on past the houses. Two
minutes down, you're overlooking the cerulean sea,
across to Albania. This marvellous view remains with
you for the rest of the hike. The track zigzags lazily
down to the sea. There are no turn-offs. Sea squill, a
lovely sight with its flowering white stem, is sprinkled
liberally across the hillside. Nearing the sea, *Cardo-
patium corymbosum* — a tall thistle with clustered
flowerheads — competes with mullein stalks for height.

Sandy Kalamaki Beach appears over to the left. Soon
after, the track enters a scattering of bushes and laurels.
Ignore a track off left. Fifty minutes downhill you meet
the road, just above **Seki Bay** (**5h10min**), a pretty little
cove concealed by cypress trees. This is an ideal spot
for a dip; if you stop here, allow at least 10 minutes to
reach your bus shelter. It's along to the left, before
Kalamaki Beach (**5h20min**).

8 NIMFES • MONI AG TRIADA • KLIMATIA

See map on reverse of touring map

Distance/time: 13km/8mi; 3h55min

Grade: moderate, with a steep descent of 100m/330ft to the valley floor (special care needed if wet) and an ascent of 350m/1150ft from the valley to Moni Ag Triada

Equipment: walking boots or stout shoes, sunhat, sunglasses, suncream, long-sleeved shirt, long trousers, raingear, picnic, water

How to get there: Roda 🚌 to the Nimfes turn-off about 2km beyond Ag Douli; journey time 50min
To return: 🚌 from Klimatia (*not in the timetables;* departs Mon-Sat at 15.00 only)

Short walk: Nimfes — Moni Pantokrator of Nimfes — Nimfes: 5.5km/3.5mi: 2h05min. Easy; stout shoes will suffice. 🚌 as above, or 🚗 to/from Nimfes: park in the village car park, shortening the walk by 1h10min. Follow the main walk until it turns off to Ag Triada (at the 1h20min-point). Here keep right, to return to Nimfes (1h30min), then descend to the bus stop (2h05min).

Alternative walk: Nimfes — Moni Ag Triada — Klimatia: 8.5km/ 5.3mi; 2h45min. Moderate, with a steepish climb of about 275m/ 900ft to the monastery. From the fountain in Nimfes, cross the road and continue up the road branching off almost opposite the fountain. A little over five minutes along, you join the main walk at the 1h20min-point. Pick up the notes opposite.

This walk calls at two of the island's little-visited *monis,* each in a different setting. Moni Pantokrator of Nimfes sits concealed in a hillside cypress wood, high above a lush valley. Moni Ag Triada adorns a cone-shaped hill with a wonderful view across the olive-studded north. You head from a luxuriant valley full of gardens and trees up to the drier, stonier, olive-clad slopes. Climbing to the summit of a rocky peak, you're surrounded by soft pink heather and shiny-leafed strawberry trees. Descending back into the olive groves, you pass the sad remains of a holm oak bosket — few remain on the island.

Start out at the NIMFES JUNCTION on the Roda road. Head straight up to **Nimfes (35min)**. This village, a kind combination of new and old, sprawls across a ridge. Keep right at the fork by a memorial and a church. A few minutes further on, the sound of gushing water announces a five-spouted fountain below the road. The turn-off for Moni Pantokrator of Nimfes lies 40m/yds further on, just past the public garden. Branch off right on a wide concrete lane. Four minutes up, head right along a track through olive groves. Ignore the lane off right a minute along and a track off left minutes later. About 15 minutes from Nimfes you come to a chapel with a sprinkling of chestnut trees around it. Take the

76

path to the right of the chapel; a minute downhill, you're at the monastery **Pantokrator of Nimfes** (**55min**; Picnic 8).

Continuing on, go down the steps leading out of the grounds, coming to a spring a minute below. Scramble up behind the spring and have a look at the tiny cave chapel. Descending into the valley, the way passes the spring and curves to the right. Two minutes later, at a faint fork, drop down to the left, soon reaching the flat along the stream. You cross a faint track, and then the way swings right to cross the stream. Coming to a farm track on the far side, turn right. About 15 minutes along the track, at a junction, keep right. Ignore two turn-offs to the left, cross a small bridge, then ignore another turn-off to the left.

Coming out on the NIMFES ROAD (**1h20min**), head left for Agia Triada. *(Here the Short walk turns right, back to Nimfes, and the Alternative walk joins the main walk.)* Almost at once, pass the football pitch and continue ahead, ignoring the concrete track rising to the right. The valley continues on towards the bulky mass of Pantokrator. Just over five minutes along, the way forks. Go right, climbing the slope. Another steep ascent lies before you, up a rough gravel track. The hillside below is like an arboretum. A tiny spring sits on the right some

Moni Pantokrator of Nimfes (Picnic 8)

minutes uphill; across the way there's a water catch-
ment tank. Just above it, fork left, climbing gradually.
Ignore a track off to the right 10 minutes uphill, and another off to the left 10 minutes later. Keep to this main,
shady track until, around 50 minutes uphill, you meet a
junction where you go right. From here the chapel is
visible on the summit. The track passes through olive
groves and shortly emerges into hillside scrub. When
the track veers off to the right around the hillside,
continue straight ahead uphill on a path. This path, the
frayed remnants of an old track, circles the hillside to
the left. Around 20 minutes up, the path leads into a
driveway, which you follow up to a motorable track.
Turn right uphill to the peak, crowned by **Moni Ag
Triada** (**2h50min**). From here you overlook the long,
gently curving bay at Roda. There are benches at the
moni to relax on but, unfortunately, there are two
yappy dogs that will give you no peace. Try the bench
at the back of the monastery.

Leaving, return on the same track, following it all the
way to Klimatia. The Theapondinisi Islands come into
sight, barely visible in a summer haze. A little over 10
minutes down, ignore a track turning off to the right
and, 10 minutes later, ignore a fork to the left. Coming
into the outskirts of **Klimatia**, you meet the road just by
the BUS STOP (**3h55min**). If you've missed the three
o'clock bus, walk on to the main Roda/Corfu road,
40 minutes away, for the Roda/Corfu bus.

9 TROUMPETA • SOKRAKI • SPARTILAS • (PYRGI)

See map on reverse of touring map

Distance/time: 10.5km/6.5mi; 2h55min

Grade: easy walking on a gravel track, with just one short stretch on slightly overgrown paths

Equipment: walking boots or stout shoes with ankle support, sunhat, sunglasses, suncream, long-sleeved shirt, long trousers, picnic, water, swimwear, cardigan, raingear

How to get there: 🚌 (Roda or Sidari bus) to Troumpeta; journey time 35min
To return: 🚌 from Spartilas (journey time 40min) or Pyrgi/Ipsos (journey time 25min)

Short walks

1 Troumpeta to Sokraki: 5km/3mi; 1h15min. Easy; all along a track; equipment and access as main walk; return by 🚌 from Sokraki. Follow the main walk to Sokraki.

2 Sokraki to Spartilas: 5.3km/3.3mi; 1h10min. Grade and equipment as main walk. Only one suitable outgoing bus a day to Sokraki, at 14.00 (not Sundays/holidays). Follow the main walk from Sokraki (the 1h10min-point); return by bus as main walk.

I f you speak a little Greek, then the local people you meet on this walk will love you. The older country folk are still extremely hospitable. But *you* have to make the first move, as they rightly think that most tourists who visit Corfu can't speak a word of their language. Your route trails along the spine of an abrupt escarpment wall stretching from east to west, severing the head of the island. The views stretch both northward and to the south, from subdued rolling countryside to a bright, curvaceous coastline. This is rural Corfu at its best.

Start off in the hamlet of **Troumpeta**, just at the top of the pass (where the bus stops). Head back south along the road towards Corfu Town. Some 50m/yds downhill, fork left on a wide gravel track climbing the face of the escarpment. This track will lead you to Sokraki. Early on in the climb, you're overlooking the central lowlands and, further east, the noticeable hayfields of the Ropa Plain. Liapades, over to the right, is the first village to appear. Shortly after, Doukades creeps into sight. Some **15min** uphill, the panorama extends to the north (Picnic 9). On a clear day you can see the Theapondinisi Islands: Othoni (the largest), Erikoussa (over to the right) and Sanothraki — all inhabited and, as yet, not a trace of tourism exists on them.

Heading up the spine of the ridge, you come upon fallow plots. Approaching the **30min**-mark, come alongside a small flat area with a few surrounding terraces. The crest is speckled with rock, which turns to a burning white under the relentless midday sun. The remains of a homestead sit on the edge of the flat area, almost obscured by trees and holly oak bushes. Closer to the track lies a WELL, but the water is only for animals.

Continuing towards Sokraki, pass by orchards, vineyards, and small gardens — all with backdrops of maquis. Cypress trees dot the hillsides. Ignore the track branching off left (**40min**). Two minutes later, some farm dwellings appear on a wooded hillock above the track. Just around the bend, the bold mound of Pantokrator fills the view. Villagers pass by, usually with laden donkeys, a goat or two wandering along in front, and a dog trailing far behind. Shortly after passing a track forking off left, you round a bend and look across a cultivated basin to Sokraki. Entering the village, the way becomes tarred. Just after passing a road off to the right, you snatch a view of the gulf and then bear left along the road through the centre of **Sokraki** (**1h10min**), passing a number of cafés. (*Short walk 1 ends here, and Short walk 2 begins here.*)

Ignore the road turning off to the right; leave Sokraki on the main road. On a bend just outside the village,

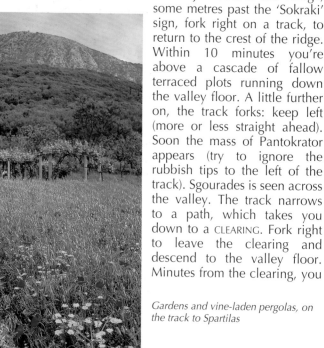

some metres past the 'Sokraki' sign, fork right on a track, to return to the crest of the ridge. Within 10 minutes you're above a cascade of fallow terraced plots running down the valley floor. A little further on, the track forks: keep left (more or less straight ahead). Soon the mass of Pantokrator appears (try to ignore the rubbish tips to the left of the track). Sgourades is seen across the valley. The track narrows to a path, which takes you down to a CLEARING. Fork right to leave the clearing and descend to the valley floor. Minutes from the clearing, you

Gardens and vine-laden pergolas, on the track to Spartilas

pass between terraced fields amidst the scrub and, just after, a farm building appears on the left, partially hidden by the scrub. Keep to the main path as it bears right here, but ignore all faint paths branching off to the right.

The path descends to the VALLEY FLOOR via a couple of stone terracing walls. Head halfway across the floor of the valley; a grove of cypress trees stands across from you. Here, turn right along the valley. The path gradually curves over to the right-hand side of the valley. Ten minutes along, you pass between a WATER CISTERN and a STONE HUT. Again, the way bears slightly right, as you descend through overgrown and abandoned plots, hemmed in by trees and bushes. Some of the terraces you clamber down while following this beautiful, wooded path are quite high. Emerging from the scrub, you come into farmland — olive groves, fruit trees, vegetable plots, and vineyards. The way now heads across the right-hand side of the valley. A minute along, you come to a concrete wall below a vineyard, on the far side of which stands a pergola. Swing right in front of the wall, to reach a TRACK just above (**2h15min**). Go left on the track, to make for Spartilas, 40 minutes away. No turn-offs are necessary, so ignore the fork to the left in 10 minutes, followed by a fork to the right.

Vineyards occupy the gently-sloping inclines. When you meet a tarred road, turn right. A minute downhill, you have an excellent view of Spartilas from a parking area on the right. **Spartilas** (**2h55min**) is set in a crease in the mountain wall, with a superb outlook over the gulf. The BUS STOP (unmarked) is just past the community office ('ΚΟΙΝΟΤΙΚΟΝ ΓΡΑΦΕΙΟΝ ΣΠΑΡΤΙΛΑ') on your right.

But if you still have some bounce left in you, why not walk on to Pyrgi, just over an hour away? The route alternates between road and cobbled path and is a pleasant descent if there isn't too much traffic. To get there, turn right downhill on the alley just before the community office. Fork left at the back of the building and then keep down to the right. Two minutes from the road, when the way becomes a wide lane, take the wide steps down to the right. Continue down the steps until you reach the road. From here, keep descending on the short-cut path, cutting loops off the road. The last piece of path takes you down to the road at the sea front in Pyrgi, where you find the bus stop (1h05min from Spartilas).

10 PEROULADES • CAPE DRASTIS • PEROULADES • AVLIOTES • MAGOULADES

Distance/time: 12km/7.5mi; 3h55min

Grade: easy to moderate; overall climbs totalling about 200m/650ft, with one fairly steep ascent of about 80m/260ft, lasting 10 minutes

Equipment: walking boots or shoes with good grip, sunhat, sunglasses, suncream, long-sleeved shirt, long trousers, cardigan, raingear, swimwear, picnic, water

How to get there: 🚌 to Peroulades; journey time 1h20min
To return: 🚌 from Magoulades; journey time 1h10min

Short walks

1 Peroulades — Cape Drastis — Peroulades: 2.8km/1.8mi; 1h10min. Grade and equipment as above; 🚌 or 🚗 to/from Peroulades (park in the parking area just below the village square). Include the local beach as well and make it a 'beach day'. Follow the main walk to the cape and back.

2 Magoulades — Moni Ipsili and Moni Ithamini — Magoulades: 6.5km/4mi; 1h40min. Easy; stout shoes will suffice. 🚗 to/from Magoulades (bus times are inconvenient); park near the church at the top of the village. Follow the road opposite the church, walking all the way along the top of the ridge. In 30min join a track coming from the left. In less than a minute you are at the junction for the monasteries. Pick up the main walk at the 2h50min-point and follow it to the end.

T he magnificent bluffs of Cape Drastis will take your breath away. Minuscule off-shore islands, finely etched with circles, look fresh off a potters' wheel. A tiny cove, set deep in the cliff-hanging cape, assures peaceful bathing (apart from Sundays and holidays) for those who seek solitude. But if you feel safer with sand and people, then the equally impressive village beach will serve you fine. Later in the walk, you head into the quiet inland hills, under the shade of the ubiquitous olive tree, to the walled-in silence of two monasteries.

The walk begins at the parking area/bus stop just below the village square in **Peroulades**. Walk some 30m/yds along the main road further into the village. Then turn right up a concrete lane signposted 'CAPE DRASTIS'. Head up to the church and school (in the same grounds), then keep straight uphill, climbing a track past the left-hand side of the school. Cross the brow of the hill, ignoring the track joining you from the right. Now begin descending towards the sea and smell the tang in the air. Albania, stretching across the horizon in front of you, is a continuous line of mountains.

Some 50m/yds downhill, take steps up left to a viewpoint, but be very *careful* here: without warning, you'll find yourself on the edge of a precipice, where dazzling, pearl-white cliffs slice their way around the point. Past the viewpoint, ignore the farm track branching off

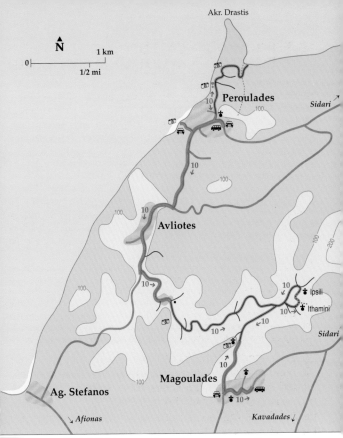

inland; keep straight on. The view par excellence over this beauty spot, shown on page 84, unfolds three minutes later. You look out over an arc of islets just offshore. Follow the main track downhill, to the COVE at **Cape Drastis** (**30min**). This is an excellent swimming spot, as it is not too deep and it's easy to scramble out of the water. The backdrop is an impressive white wall rising straight up out of a crystal-blue sea.

Return to **Peroulades** (**1h05min**) on the same track and turn right below the school, along the village road. Tourism has barely touched this village. Three minutes along, take the first tarred lane branching off to the right, signposted 'LOGAS BEACH/TAVERNA SUNSET'. Barely a minute along, turn right on a concrete lane. The restaurant lies a minute along and, a few hundred metres/yards further on, you're at a parking area overlooking the sea. Just below you (but still out of sight) stretches a spectacular beach. Only a collar of sand separates the sea from the base of the high cliffs. A steep path plonks you down onto the beach in two minutes.

Return from the beach to the turn-off and head right towards Avliotes, following a winding country road between fields. At the junction, a good five minutes along, fork right (to continue more or less straight ahead). Some 25 minutes from the beach, meet the main road and head uphill to the right, through **Avliotes** (**1h40min**). A good five minutes sees you at the far end of this unprepossessing village where, at a junction, you head left towards Ag Stefanos (signposted).

Ignore the first turn-off to the left but, 10 minutes from Avliotes, turn off left on a surfaced lane (the second left turn you come to). The way climbs up over a ridge. *Zorro* — masked sheep with uneven black socks — often graze the inclines here. Ignoring a track off right, you enter a hamlet. Three minutes later, when the tarred road ends (below the last house), continue on a track striking off right, to climb the side of a ridge.

The 'view par excellence' over Cape Drastis

Arilas and Gravia Island appear through an open V in the encircling ridges. Crossing the crest, ignore a fork to the right, then another to the left. Soon pass above a trackside dump. Avliotes, a blend of pinkish buildings stepping the crest of a ridge on the far side of the valley, catches your eye. It's far more attractive when seen from afar.

A four-way junction comes your way half an hour up the track. Keep straight ahead, to cross to the right side of the crest, continuing the ascent. A little over five minutes uphill, join a concrete road coming from the right and follow it to the left. (On your return, you will take this road to Magoulades.) A minute later come to the turn-off for the monasteries (**2h50min**). Moni Ipsili is to the left; Moni Ithamini to the right. Head right. Just after turning off, fork left on a narrow track. Five minutes later, at a junction, head up to the left. **Moni Ithamini** (**3h**) — a nunnery snuggled into a hillside hollow under an umbrella of unpruned citrus trees, loquats and elms, looks deserted; the gardens are overgrown.

From the nunnery take the path to the left of the building. Half a minute uphill, your path strikes off left up the hillside and climbs steeply to the top of the crest, bearing right and then uphill to **Moni Ipsili** (**3h05min**), the monks' hermitage. Moni Ipsili boasts some valuable icons and paintings, but they are kept locked away.

To continue the walk, follow the track leaving the *moni*. At the junction just below it, turn left. Keeping straight on, return to the Magoulades turn-off, a minute below the fork you took to the nunnery. Head left. No turn-offs are required, but you might like to detour to an isolated church up on your right some 10 minutes along, to enjoy the views. After the way becomes tarred, you soon emerge on a road descending through **Magoulades**. A church stands opposite. Turn left and pass through this very colourful village. Less than 20 minutes downhill, at a roundabout just below the village, come to the BUS STOP (**3h55min**) for buses to Corfu Town.

11 VISTONAS • PRINILAS • AG GEORGIOS BEACH • CAPE ARILLA • AFIONAS

Photos pages 10-11, 28   **Distance/time:** 10.5km/6.5mi; 3h15min

Grade: moderate to strenuous, with an initial descent of 400m/1300ft (one short steep stretch) and an ascent of 150m/500ft at the end. The paths are slippery in wet weather.

Equipment: walking boots or stout shoes with good grip and ankle support, sunhat, sunglasses, suncream, long-sleeved shirt, cardigan, long trousers, rainwear, swimwear, picnic, water

How to get there: 🚌 to Paleokastritsa and taxi from there to the Prinilas turn-off, just outside Vistonas. Or take the 7am Krini bus (not Sundays or holidays) as far as the Prinilas turn-off — the first junction before Vistonas (on the bus route); journey time 50min.

To return: 🚌 from Afionas; journey time 2h15min. The departure time of this bus varies by as much as 30 minutes; arrive early! Or, when you reach Afionas, telephone at one of the cafés for a Sidari taxi, to take you to Sidari, for better bus connections.

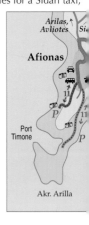

Short walk: Afionas — Cape Arilla — Afionas: 2km/1.3mi; 45min. Moderate descent/climb of 100m/330ft; wear stout shoes. 🚗 to and from Afionas; park in the village, at the end of the road, keeping well clear of the square where the bus turns round. Pick up the main walk at the 2h05min point and follow it to the end.

Alternative walk: Paleokastritsa — Vistonas — Prinilas — Ag Georgios Beach — Cape Arilla — Afionas: 14km/8.8mi; 4h10min. Strenuous and long; equipment as main walk. 🚌 to Paleokastritsa; return as main walk. Follow *Walk 12* (page 89) to Lakones (40min), where Walk 12 turns right through the village. Turn *left* here. Five minutes along, leave the road, climbing a path on the right (opposite 'Alki's Artist Olive Wood Production'). A little over 10 minutes up, a greenhouse is visible below in the valley floor. The track ascending behind it will take you out of the valley. To reach the track, continue along the main path until you are across the valley from the greenhouse. Ignore the path forking off right here but, 40m/yds further on, leave the main path and swing sharply back to the left, to pick up a path that leads to the track, two minutes away. Remember to say 'ay**pee**traytay na pera**hso may**sa **ah**poh toe **ayk**teema **sas**?' (please may I pass through your property?) when crossing someone's land. This track takes you to another track, where you turn right. Ignore a track off to the right; continue up to the main road and turn left. Less than 15 minutes uphill, just past the village church in Vistonas, turn off right for Prinilas (1h10min). This is where Walk 11 starts: follow the notes below from beginning to end.

In recent years, a couple of stretches along this walk have been tarred. But I enjoy the views so much that I decided not to change the route. This walk is all about the spectacular setting of Ag Georgios Beach. Descending into the scooped-out bay of Ag Georgiou, you look down into a limpid green sea. Cape Arilla, the sharp rocky arm completing the bay, is the final leg of the hike, where you visit the wild twin coves of Port Timone.

The walk starts at the PRINILAS TURN-OFF, just outside **Vistonas**. A church stands above the road to the right. Walk along the road towards Prinilas, at the outset looking over onto Makarades (the closer village) and Krini. A few minutes along, you're circling a sunken cultivated basin. Rocky hilltops surround you. If a nor'-westerly is blowing, you'll take the full brunt of it as you cross this ridge. Around **15min** along there is a striking view over Ag Georgiou Bay and the gentle hills of the northwest. Beyond the cape, stepping their way into the horizon, lie the Theapondinisi Islands and a couple of islets. The ongoing path is visible across the bay, cut into the sheer sides of the arm of the cape.

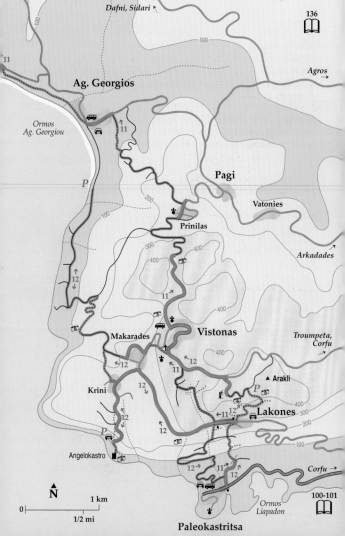

The road reverts to gravel, and soon you look down onto the roof tiles of the pretty village of Prinilas. Join another gravel road coming from the left (**35min**) and follow it to the right, keeping on the main track.

Orchards filled with almond trees crowd around **Prinilas** (**50min**). Entering the village, keep an eye out for a church below the road. Just past it, branch off left down a concrete lane. It drops straight down onto another lane: cross it and continue down past the houses, keeping left, until you meet the road again two minutes later. Turn left. Some 40m/yds further on, take the first left — a farm lane. Pass a house and find yourselves immersed in orchards, vineyards, and olive groves. Within 10 minutes ignore a track forking off left. Ignore, too, the faint fork off to the left a few minutes later. But two minutes beyond this second turn-off, leave the main track: strike off left on a track that quickly becomes a path and descends the nose of a steep ridge. The way widens into a track and meets the road, where you turn left to **Ag Georgios Beach** (**1h20min**).

Head right along the beach for 30 minutes, to the road that ascends to Afionas. A steep 15-minute climb takes you up to a T-junction; turn left. Ten minutes later you're in the square at **Afionas** (**2h05min**). Its strategic setting makes Afionas prone to winds, but the villagers must think the views compensate for the inconvenience.

Now make for Cape Arilla: standing with your back to the church door, head off into the alley 10m/yds to the left. (A sign 'DIONYSOS TAVERNA', is just inside the alley.) After 70m/yds, turn left on a path. Follow the main path all the way, ignoring any forks to the right. From this side of the bay, the view is equally appealing. Inland, big bursts of forest-green hills roll one upon the other. The crystal-clear sea becomes hypnotic. Rounding the hillside, the two bright little coves shown on pages 10-11 shine up at you (Picnic 11). In ancient times the larger cove was known as the Tiller's Port (**Port Timone**; **2h35min**), where boats came to shelter from approaching storms. You can outwit the wind too: should a strong northerly be blowing, shelter in the bay-side cove; if it's a sou'-westerly, stick to the port side. A collar of land separates the two. The promontory joined to this tiny necklace of land is tightly woven in maquis.

Back at the square in **Afionas** (**3h15min**), be sure to take the wide path opposite the church, to climb to the spine of the ridge. See notes for Picnic 11 on page 11.

12 PALEOKASTRITSA • LAKONES • MT ARAKLI • MAKARADES • AG GEORGIOU BAY • ANGELOKASTRO • PALEOKASTRITSA

See map page 86-87; see also photographs page 18-19, 31

Distance/time: 19.5km/12mi; 6h10min

Grade: strenuous, with overall ascents/descents of 730m/2400ft; possibility of vertigo at Angelokastro

Equipment: walking boots, sunhat, suncream, sunglasses, long-sleeved shirt, long trousers, raingear, swimwear, picnic, water

How to get there and return: 🚌 (journey time 40min) or 🚗 to/from Paleokastritsa; park in the car park below the monastery

Short walks

1 Paleokastritsa — Lakones — Mt Arakli — Paleokastritsa: 5km/3mi; 2h20min. Strenuous, with overall ascent/descent of 400m/1300ft; equipment and access as main walk. Follow the main walk to the track at the foot of Mt Arakli (1h15min), then return the same way.

2 Paleokastritsa — Lakones — Angelokastro — Paleokastritsa: 5.8km/3.5mi; 2h50min. Moderate-strenuous, with overall ascent/descent of 330m/1075ft (the ascent to Lakones and the castle is steep). Equipment and access as main walk. This is a popular route with 'Landscapers'. Follow the main walk to Lakones and from there walk along the road to Krini. At Krini, pick up the main walk again at the 4h30min-point, to go on to Angelokastro and return to Paleokastritsa.

P aleokastritsa is Corfu's tourist mecca. But, fortunately, tourist development has not yet disfigured this natural asset. Here the hike begins and ends. Along old cobbled paths, you ascend the flanks of Mt Arakli for unsurpassed views of the Bay of Liapades. Returning to the coast, you climb to the impenetrable fortress of Angelokastro. Its few skeletal remains have little to offer, but its sheer-sided perch will leave you in awe — if not fright — as you peer down into a milky-green sea 330m/1075ft below. Midway, a detour down a cliff-hanging donkey trail (the old northeast road), drops you into the exquisite horseshoe bay of Ag Georgiou.

The walk begins at the CAR PARK/BUS TERMINUS in **Paleokastritsa**. Walk back along the main road for about 200m/yds. Then take the first turn-off left, just beyond another parking area and opposite the TAVERNA CALM. Some 70m/yds uphill, fork right on a lane. This is where the real ascent begins. Continue up this road for about 10 minutes — or until you see a wide path climbing up to the left. (This is at a point where the road briefly flattens out, and there is a water pipe at the side of the road.) Straight into the path, it forks, but both branches rejoin after a few metres/yards. Keep straight uphill. Soon you're on a lovely old stone-paved path. A few minutes up, a path joins from the right; keep

Top: a corridor in the rocky hillsides frames our view to Ag Georgiou Bay. Bottom: the cliff-hanging donkey trail (the old northeast road) descends in zigzags.

straight on, under the shade of olive trees. Half-moons of terracing stretch across the hillside. Midway up to Lakones, you enter a passageway slicing up through a vertical rock face. Out of the passage and back into terraced hillsides, you cross a track, and then enter **Lakones**. The path veers right, to where an alley cuts across in front of you. Turn left up the alley and, on meeting the ROAD (**40min**), turn right. *(But for Short walk 2, turn left.)*

After 200m/yds, climb steps up to the left (just past a butcher's shop). In two minutes come to a T-junction. Turn right uphill — this is the path up the SLOPES OF **Mt Arakli** (Picnic 12a). Ignore a faint turn-off to the left. About 15 minutes from the road, turn left uphill on a cobbled path. This takes you up to the cleavage in the top of the ridge, where you are rewarded with unparalleled views over the Bay of Liapades. Perhaps the guide books aren't exaggerating when they claim this to be one of the finest views in all of Europe. Vivid turquoise coves cut their way around a hilly coastline of wooded headlands, and craggy bluffs tumble off into a rich blue sea. Lakones, a thick line of dappled brown rooftops, rests on a pause in the ridge.

The path disappears into maquis as it crosses the flat area between the hills on either side. Keep straight across the flat area, in three minutes meeting a TRACK (**1h15min**). Turn left here, leaving the summit of Mt Arakli off to the right. A minute up the track there is a more expansive view, which includes the Ropa Valley and Angelokastro over to the right. After enjoying the view, continue on past some radar equipment. *(Those doing Short walk 1 return the same way now to Paleokastritsa.)*

Descending to the road, bear left. Krini, which you visit later on in the hike, is over to the left. Barely 15 minutes along the road, and entering **Vistonas**, you can take a short-cut path to the left: it starts just past the sign, 'VISTONAS', beside a SHRINE at the side of the road. It takes you past a church. From the church keep straight downhill and rejoin the road. Then go left for some 40m/yds and rejoin the path. (But if it's overgrown remain on the road.) Back on the road, turn left and come to the MAKARADES JUNCTION (**2h10min**). Make a dash to the right, before the stall-keepers catch you! Continue through **Makarades** until you come to a concrete lane cutting across in front of you (just past the last houses and a cafeneion; a field lies on the far side of this lane). Head right along the lane. The concrete only lasts for two minutes, then gravel comes underfoot. A few minutes down, a neat path, bordered by tired stone walls, runs into the track from the left. Keep this path in mind — it is your way to Krini on the return.

Ten minutes downhill, the track comes to a dead end — for vehicles. Ahead lies the most unexpected sight: the path (the old road to the village of Ag Georgios, now only for pedestrians and donkeys) cuts through a corridor in the hillside rock. Once through it, you're virtually 'hanging' out over glorious Ag Georgiou Bay; the piercing blue sea, trimmed in turquoise, shimmers below. Clinging to the escarpment, the way leisurely descends, and then — time running out — twists and turns in panic to reach the bottom. Ten minutes down, you reach a gravel road and follow it downhill to the coast. On the descent look across the translucent bay to Cape Arilla (Walk 11) and the Theapondinisi Islands. At the junction that follows, keep right. This is a beautiful stroll, looking through the olive trees down onto the green sea. A number of tracks lead down to the sea; you might like to explore any one of them. About 45 minutes after leaving the path, you reach **Ag Georgios Beach** (**3h25min**; Picnic 12b). Here the walk turns around and heads back the same way. (But first you might like to visit the village of Ag Georgios, a further ten minutes along the track, a detour not included in the overall timing.)

The return involves an uphill slog lasting just over an hour. Remember to turn off for Krini up the path flanked by tired stone walls that you noted on your descent from Makarades. It will now be on your right, with a sign, 'SUNSET TAVERNA', just where it starts. This beautiful path through garden plots and vineyards leads up to **Krini (4h30min)**. At the T-junction with a narrow alley just inside the village, turn left. You come to a road with a tree in the middle of it (the village centre); turn right here. Head through the village, continuing straight on along the road. Two minutes later, when you reach a second junction, keep right (more or less straight on).

Ten minutes downhill you're at the foot of a stumpy tower of scrub-covered rock, crowned by the castle ruins. Take the path leading off the parking area, and follow it to the top, keeping right at the fork three minutes up. From **Angelokastro** (Picnic 12c) the views are superb. You look along the escarpment wall as it slides off into a bay indented with sandy coves. On a clear day you can see all the way to Corfu Town — hence the strategic importance of this castle.

On the return to Krini, you can use paths to cut out some bends in the road (the paths are shown on the map). Back in the centre of **Krini** (where the tree stands in the middle of the road), keep right (more or less straight ahead). At the junction that follows, turn right on the main road. Some 20 minutes along (about five minutes past Taverna Bellavista), descend steps alongside a shop on the right (ALKI'S ARTIST OLIVE WOOD PRODUCTION; **5h35min**). Two minutes down, ignore a faint fork off to the left. On coming onto a track, follow it downhill. Remain on this track some 40 minutes, all the way down to **Paleokastritsa**. The BUS STOP is a couple of minutes long to the right (**6h10min**).

13 PALEOKASTRITSA • LIAPADES • GIANADES • ROPA PLAIN • SGOMBOU

See map pages 100-101; see also photograph pages 32-33

Distance/time: 18.5km/11.5mi; 5h

Grade: easy, but long, with gradual ascents of about 350m/1150ft overall. There is a short, very awkward descent down a cleft near the start of the walk (dangerous if wet); less agile walkers should avoid this by starting out from Liapades, at the 40min-point.

Equipment: walking boots or stout shoes with good grip, sunhat, sunglasses, suncream, long-sleeved shirt, long trousers, raingear, swimwear, picnic, water

How to get there: 🚌 (journey time 35min) or 🚗 to Paleokastritsa; alight from the bus at Paleokastritsa Camping; park as near as possible to the camping site.
To return: 🚌 from Sgombou (Paleokastritsa bus), to Corfu Town (journey time 20min), or to back to Paleokastritsa Camping for your car

Short walks

1 Paleokastritsa — Liapades — Gianades: 8.5km/5.3mi; 2h20min; Easy; equipment, access *by bus* as main walk; return by 🚌 from Gianades (not Sundays/holidays). Follow the main walk to Gianades.

2 Paleokastritsa — Bovina Beach — Paleokastritsa: 5km/3mi; 1h40min. Easy; equipment, access as main walk; return on the same bus or by car. Follow the main walk for a little over 30min — as far as the fork just after you leave the road at Villa Birlis. At the fork, bear right. Yellow arrows indicate the route. After heading behind a couple of buildings, the path swings abruptly left. Just after this, turn off to the right, and remain on this path, descending through a bosket of kermes oak, to the beach, ignoring paths off to the right. There are two caves on the beach, one of them quite impressive. Return the same way.

Alternative walks

1 Paleokastritsa — Liapades — Cape Ag Iliodoros — Liapades — Paleokastritsa: 12km/7.5mi; 3h40min. Fairly strenuous, with a steep ascent of 220m/720ft on the return from the cove. Equipment and access as main walk. Follow the main walk as far as the country road just above Liapades. Two minutes up this road (the 50min-point), turn off right on a track. Quickly coming to a fork, go left. Now ignore all tracks forking off right; remain on this track all the way to an isolated little cove on Cape Ag Iliodoros, 45 minutes downhill. Stupendous views across Liapades Bay await you. Return the same way.

2 Paleokastritsa — Liapades — Marmaro Hills — Liapades — Paleokastritsa: 13km/8mi; 3h40min. Easy-moderate, with a gradual ascent of 250m/820ft. Equipment and access as main walk. This wonderful ramble soaks up the countryside. Flowers (in autumn, *Sternbergia*, cyclamen, squill and crocuses) lie so thickly in some hillside pockets you'll think you're in a garden. Follow the main walk as far as the fork at the roadside shrine (55min). Here go right (more or less straight ahead). Walking through beautiful olive groves, circle the Marmaro Hills, terraced in tired stone walls and soft with grass. Stay on this main track until you meet a junction (1h35min); keep left here. In five minutes, head left once again. At the next junction, 20 minutes later (where there is an unfinished concrete block building on the right), turn right and then immediately left. Around 15 minutes later, ignore a track forking off to the right. Approaching the next

93

junction (2h25min), you encounter the splendid pocket of *Sternbergia* shown on page 96. Keep right, soon enjoying a view of the escarpment wall cutting across the north of the island. Within the next 20 minutes meet a track cutting across in front of you, and turn left downhill to Liapades. On entering the village, continue down to the right on a lane. When you meet a narrow village road, follow it a short way left uphill, then take the first right and, at the end of this alley, descend to the right, to the village square (3h). Returning on the outward route, keep left at the bottom of the square.

M eander through mossy olive groves to the sound of chirping birds and, if you're unlucky, the blast of a shotgun — someone after those chirping birds. Cross a plain squared by ditches and cushioned in grass, with not an olive tree in sight. Plod along an open, shallow valley littered with scrub and trees. In spring, orchids, stars of Bethlehem, anemones and wild geraniums adorn this countryside. In autumn, the dry and faded, rocky hillsides are embellished with cyclamen and *Sternbergia,* the fields carpeted in squill and crocuses.

The walk starts at PALEOKASTRITSA CAMPING, on the edge of **Paleokastritsa**. Head back along the main road towards Corfu Town. Some 80 paces beyond SUPER-MARKET ARIS (just past a scooter rental shop), bear right on a concrete lane. At the end of the lane pick up a path heading between two houses (signposted to the 'ACAPULCO' swimming pool). A couple of minutes across an olive grove, drop down onto a concrete lane, where the advertised pool is to your right. Head left on the lane for about 12m/yds, then climb some steps on the right. At the top of the steps continue along the path to the right, soon entering hillside scrub. Three minutes from the lane, you look straight down into a cleft in the ridge. Although only about 2m/6ft deep, it's steep and makes for an awkward descent. *Care and all fours are required. If at all wet it's dangerous! Don't use the rope here unless you're absolutely sure it's properly secured, and strong enough to hold your weight!*

A steep descent on a path follows. Soon you overlook a cove set in rock walls. Ignore the path

Bovina Beach (Short walk 2)

ascending to the left. The path emerges in the grounds of the Elli Beach Hotel. Pass the pool to get down to the BEACH (**20min**). Follow the road uphill from the beach for about 10 minutes, then climb steps up to the right (just past Villa Birlis, a small apartment block). Two minutes up the way forks and you go left. *(But for Short walk 2, go right here for Bovina Beach.)* On reaching a road, turn left along it. Almost immediately, at a fork, head right.

Come into **Liapades** (**40min**), with its lovely manorial homes, handsome arched doorways and courtyards. Go straight ahead to the square (ignore turnings uphill to the right). With the church on the right, leave the square along the alley ahead (with sign forbidding entry for vehicles). Two minutes uphill, at a T-junction (just beyond a Venetian manor on the left), turn left on a wide concrete path. A good five minutes up from the square, a country road cuts across in front of you; turn right. Two minutes along the road, where a track forks off to the right, keep left on the road (**50min**). *(But Alternative walk 1 heads right on the track.)*

Some five minutes later, at the next fork (there is a SHRINE just beyond it; **55min**), keep left. *(But for Alternative walk 2, head right here.)* The way soon reverts to gravel. Within the next 15 minutes, leave the main track, which turns sharp left, and continue ahead on a lesser track, to ascend a gentle ridge. In 10 minutes the track fizzles out at a stone RUIN. Continue straight ahead

Left: autumn-flowering cyclamen; right: Sternbergia

off the track, following a faint path across an olive grove (*don't* take the wider path heading right). A minute downhill come onto a farm track and turn right. Several minutes along the track, at a T-junction, turn left. Continue to ascend, now on the opposite side of the ridge.

The Ropa Valley comes into view through a V in the hills. Flat, herbaceous, and dotted with a few trees, it makes a complete transition in the landscape. Slightly further on, you look straight across the centre of the island. A descent follows, down a shallow side-valley. Some five minutes from the last junction, join a track on a bend and follow it to the right, heading down into the side-valley. (*Don't* take the fainter track immediately to the right.) In the distance stand the black mounds of Mt Ag Georgios near Vatos (Walk 15) and Ag Deka (Walk 16). Ten minutes along, ignore a faint track off to the left and, five minutes later, at a junction, keep right (but *ignore* the *faint* turn-off right just before this junction). Three minutes later a track joins you from the right. Looking across the valley you can see a church, which you will soon pass. Two more junctions follow: keep left at both of them. Meeting a road, turn left. Passing the church, you meet the main road where it enters **Gianades (2h20min)**. The prettiest corner of the village, draped in bougainvillaea, is to the left.

Two minutes along the road, fork left on another road (the second turn-off left you encounter). Passing the last houses, you return to olive-wooded hillsides. When you reach a T-junction around 15 minutes downhill, keep right. *Attention* is needed five minutes later: the ditch which has been on the right-hand side of the road passes under the road and emerges on the left. As soon as you cross this culvert, swing left on a farm track and head across the **Ropa Plain**.

Five minutes along, you cross a bridge, and a faint track joins you from the right. Again, *pay attention* after five minutes: you cross a bridge (hardly noticeable, because it is so grassy) and meet a track. Cross the track *and* the deep ditch running parallel to it (there may be water in it in spring). Out of the ditch, cross another track and then another bridge. Now keep straight ahead. When the track fades out, make for the line of cypress trees not far ahead. Closer to the trees, you have to cross another couple of ditches. Then veer left, keeping in line with the cypress trees. When the line of cypresses comes to an end, continue straight ahead in the same direction. Remaining in the grassy field, pick up a path which leads to a faint track, about three minutes from the cypress trees. (In spring, when the grass is tall, this path is hardly visible.) Turn right on the track, up to the road (**3h25min**).

Turn right on the road and, after 30m/yds (just before a café), turn left on a narrow concrete lane — there is a SIGN WITH A GRASSHOPPER at the entrance. The concrete gives way to gravel, which in turn becomes tarred and cuts through a ridge. Stay on this road, which soon reverts to gravel again. You come into a very shallow valley, with an anarchy of vegetation. The escarpment wall reappears, filling the landscape to the north, with Skripero at its foot.

Some 10 minutes from the turn-off, ignore a farm track forking off left. A little over five minutes later, ignore a driveway forking off right. Here the track swings sharp left, and then sharp right, to pass through a gap in the hedge straight ahead. Continue straight on through a row of luminous pines. Then bear right. A first pond appears over on your left. **Gavrolimini** (Picnic 13), the next pond, follows, almost hidden by the surrounding cultivation. The track briefly heads between high fences. Ignore two turn-offs to the right a few minutes later. On reaching a road (tarred to the left, gravel to the right), go right. Five minutes later, you pass a track off to the left. Entering the hamlet of **Trivou-liattica** (**4h35min**), keep straight ahead. Continue north for 25 minutes, to the main Paleokastritsa road (and BUS STOP), at **Sgombou** (**5h**).

14 SGOMBOU • DOUKADES • AG SIMEON • SGOMBOU

Distance/time: 25km/15.5mi; 8h

Grade: moderate but long, the only noticeable ascent being a steep climb of 150m/500ft to Doukades and Ag Simeon. *Map-reading skill is required,* as some of the tracks and paths are hardly visible in spring. Beware of dogs running loose about 15min past Ag Noufures.

Equipment: walking boots or stout shoes with ankle support, sunhat, sunglasses, suncream, long-sleeved shirt, long trousers, raingear, picnic, plenty of water

How to get there and return: 🚌 (Paleokastritsa bus; journey time 20min) or 🚗 to/from Sgombou. Alight from the bus at the stop for the Lucciola Inn; motorists park by the side of the road near the inn.

Shorter walks

1 Sgombou — Gavrolimni Pond — Doukades — Ag Simeon — Doukades — Paleokastritsa road: 15km/9.5mi: 4h20min. Grade, equipment and access as above; return on the Paleokastritsa bus — to Corfu Town, or back to your car at Sgombou. Follow the main walk until you return to Doukades (4h05min). Leave the main walk here to return to the main road, 1km away (4h20min). Catch the bus across from the turn-off; it passes here 5min after departing Paleokastritsa.

2 Doukades — Ag Simeon — Doukades — Sgombou: 19.5km/ 12mi; 5h30min. Grade, equipment, access/return as main walk (take the Paleokastritsa bus to either Doukades turn-off; journey time 25min; travelling by car, park at the Lucciola Inn and pick up the bus there). From the bus stop, walk uphill to the village (1km/25min). Turn left at the first junction, then left again along an alley. Now pick up the main walk at the 3h-point (where the church door is on your right).

This is a hike full of bucolic charm. You pass by ponds, through thickets of tangled foliage, and cross grassy fields. On route you call at Ag Noufures, a charming abandoned monastery. An hour later, you climb an escarpment to the precariously-perched chapel of Ag Simeon, overlooking the turquoise waters of Liapades Bay. A striking panorama spreads out below you, and you can trace the route of the walk.

Start the walk in **Sgombou**. From the bus stop, cross the road, then turn right just past the mini-market, to reach the LUCCIOLA INN, a taverna (motorists should park nearby). Continue up the road that passes to the left of the inn, towards the cypress trees. Follow this road to the hamlet of **Trivouliattica** (**25min**). Here a road turns off left, but keep straight on, following more cypress trees. Close on 10 minutes later, ignore a track forking off to the right. Five minutes later, fork left on a faint track (the tarred lane to the right is your return route). In two minutes, at a fork, keep right; then ignore the faint fork to the left just afterwards. Shortly, you pass to the left of **Gavrolimni pond**, fenced off and surrounded by vegetable plots. In winter it's a good-sized pond, frequented by herons and, to a lesser extent, egrets and moorhens. Two large holly oaks at the side of the fenced track mark your approach to this pond. Crossing a broad plain, you'll see another pond over to your right (but in summer it will be dried-up).

As you head through a line of pretty pines, keep straight on along the now-faint track. After 100m/yds, the way veers sharply left, to pass in front of two buildings on the right. Another building sits back off the track over to the left. Barely two minutes through the pines, you come alongside the driveway of the house on the left. Here, turn off the track and cross the field on your right. Within a few metres/yards you will spot a track about 200m/yds ahead; make for it, passing a jumble of abandoned vehicles on the left.

Once on the farm track, head right and pass below a derelict building amidst kermes oaks, on the right. From the track, the remains of the Ag Noufures monastery are visible through the trees covering the ridge not far ahead. This is your immediate destination. Five minutes along the track, you pass a house which rubs shoulders with an old ruin set behind a high fence. Just past here, the track peters out. Pick up a path to the left of the track. It heads in the direction of the *moni*, first crossing the field ahead. Head towards the left-hand side of the field; two minutes across it, you cross a ditch and pass through a gap in the bushes. Now weave your way through the bushes and pick up one of the animal paths heading towards the monastery. In three minutes you're at **Ag Noufures (1h30min)**. The gates of the churchyard are usually open. Inside the yard it's cool and fresh.

In the grounds of Ag Noufures

To continue the walk, stand with the belfry on your left, and head north along the crest, to reach a rough dirt track. Follow it to the right and head back down into the valley. Around 10 minutes from the *moni,* the track forks. Go right (more or less straight on). An old rusty fence runs along the right-hand side of the track. Minutes later, you climb over a gate and immediately after pass very close to a farm shed. Now get out your 'Dog Dazer', or arm yourself with a stick or some stones. All hell breaks loose here, as half a dozen dogs

literally go beserk. Sometimes a couple of them may be loose.

Beyond the shed, continue on an old stone-laid trail that goes straight on. Ignore the farm track on the left. Minutes later, you join this farm track and head along it to the right. Three minutes later, a track joins from the right; keep left here. After a further three minutes, meet a private road and turn right along it. This road takes you in five minutes to the PALEOKASTRITSA ROAD (**2h**), where you turn left. The next half hour is spent on this

View over Liapades Bay from above the chapel of Ag Simeon

busy road: take care, the locals treat it like the Monte Carlo strip!

Walking towards the escarpment, you'll notice a rock face to the left. Above it sits a chapel — your eventual goal. But first make for Doukades. Turn off the main road on a sharp bend one minute past Villa Alexandra (a pretty cottage with a garden on the right, and a new house alongside it). Just beyond a roadside guard-rail (which may be covered with foliage), climb up right on a concrete lane. At the top of the rise, at a fork, keep right (more or less straight on). Ignore a fork off to the left a couple of minutes later. On meeting a tarred road, just where it reverts to gravel, turn left. This takes you in five minutes to the DOUKADES ROAD, where you turn right, immediately passing a road off to the left. Two minutes later, turn left up an alley into **Doukades**. This charming village is an artists' paradise.

A minute up, at a T-junction of paths, turn left and walk alongside a walled-in villa, with the front door of a CHURCH (**3h**) to your right. *(Shorter walk 2 and Picnic 14 join here.)* Cross a road and continue up the path. Turn off up the first narrow lane on the right. Leave the houses, following a cobbled path straight uphill. Within the first minute you cross a water pipe at an intersection, where you continue straight on. At a T-junction with a track, turn left uphill. Climbing, you have stupendous views over Doukades, towards a valley clad in silvery-grey olive groves pierced with the dark spires of cypress trees (Picnic 14). There used to be wonderful views from the crest of the escarpment, but scrub has all but blocked them out — try standing on tiptoes. Less than 15 minutes up the track, you reach a fork with a broken old sign for Ag Simeon. Descend to the left: at the end of the track, you're looking down on the chapel from the vantage point shown opposite. A minute down, at **Ag Simeon (3h40min)**, a superb cliff-top panorama awaits you. Liapades is the larger village across from you; Gardelades is to the left. The Ropa Plain, a carpet of green in spring, slides into the central hills. In the distance, beyond the rolling wooded hills, sits Corfu Town. Paleokastritsa lies among the prominent headlands below.

From the chapel, return the same way to **Doukades**. On the descent you have a good view over this picturesque village. Back at the CHURCH (**4h05min**), keep straight ahead. *(But for Shorter walk 1, turn right, down to the Paleokastritsa road.)* You descend to the Skripero road, where you turn left. Two minutes through Doukades, opposite a house with an elaborate balcony, turn right down a concrete lane. Barely a minute down, you pass a large olive tree. Just beyond it, turn right on another lane which ascends the hillside. At the next fork, a couple of minutes further uphill, go left, entering an arboretum of summer shade.

Your next turn-off requires attention. It comes up about 10 minutes beyond this last fork. Watch out for an iron shed off the track to the left, followed by a farm building on the right; a minute later, just where the track swings sharp left, fork right (straight uphill) on a very old path bounded by thick low STONE WALLS. You pass to the right of a SHED with a corrugated iron roof almost at once. Three minutes along, you're overlooking a small clearing on the edge of an olive grove. Here the path disappears into the grass. Facing the clearing, bear right (about 15°) and head across the grove. A minute across, you regain the path lined with stone walls. It leads to a faint track, which you follow to the left. Half a minute along the track, at a T-junction, turn left on another track. After 100m/yds, this track veers right, to head along the foot of a ridge. When the track fades, continue straight ahead — the track will reappear. Two minutes along the track, pass a BARN on the right. Keep straight ahead (now on a barely-discernible track), soon passing an open WELL. Ascending slightly, the track becomes clearer. When it forks, keep left (ie straight on). A minute later, at a T-junction, turn right downhill,

Teal

after 50m/yds joining a track coming from the right. Heading along to the left, squeeze by a gate across the track. The countryside is lush with trees and bushes, swallowing up the fields and plots. A few minutes along, a track joins from the left, and a minute later you join a track coming from

Green lizard

the right. Ignoring a track off left just afterwards, ascend a hill. Another track joins from the right, and then you meet a small COUNTRY ROAD (**5h15min**). Turn right and follow this road for 45 minutes, to the PALEOKASTRITSA ROAD (**6h**).

If your legs are sending you messages, you can catch a bus here. To head on, cross the road, and walk along it to the right. After 130m/yds, fork left on a track. Meeting a three-way fork, take the middle prong. Ignore a fork to the right shortly after. Tiny farms lie hidden in this scrub-covered countryside. Around 10 minutes from the road, at a first fork, go right. Just after passing faint forks to the left and then the right, the main track forks: head left uphill. Swamp and fields in a flat, tucked-away area appear through the trees below. A short climb follows. Five minutes from the fork, come to a grand old STABLE-LIKE BUILDING, with arches, on the right (**6h25min**). Ignore a track off to the left here. Continuing over the crest, you reach another fork, and again climb to the left. A few minutes afterwards, ignore faint forks to the right and left.

Two minutes later, at a flat area on a hilltop, you come to a rough clearing. Here, *attention is needed*. The track swings left, but you continue to the *right* along an overgrown track (hardly more than a path). The houses visible over to the left are your target. Two minutes further along, the way veers first left, then down to the right. Heading through the scrub, you emerge on a faint track. Ignore the faint track off to the left; keep right downhill. In five minutes join a track coming from the right and follow it to the left. A few metres/yards along, come onto a gravel road and follow it to the left, ignoring the turn-off to Ag Noufures (your outgoing route) around five minutes along. Remain on the road back to **Trivouliattica** (**7h30min**) and then walk ahead to **Sgombou** (**8h**).

Terrapin

15 GOUVIA • ROPA PLAIN • VATOS • MIRTIOTISSA BEACH • GLYFADA

See also photograph pages 32-33

Distance/time: 13.8km/8.5mi; 3h50min

Grade: recommended for experienced and adventurous walkers. While most of the walk is easy, with the only appreciable ascent being a climb of 250m/820ft above Vatos, the last stretch to the beach at Glyfada involves a steep and slippery descent of 50m/150ft.

Equipment: walking boots or shoes with good grip, sunhat, sunglasses, suncream, long-sleeved shirt, long trousers, raingear, swimwear, picnic, water

How to get there: 🚐 to Gouvia (Dasia bus; journey time 20min). Alight at Filipa's Taverna — easily spotted on your right.
To return: 🚐 from Glyfada; journey time 40min

Short walk: Vatos — Trialos — Mirtiotissa Beach — Glyfada: 5.5km/3.5mi; 2h. Moderate, with a steepish ascent of 250m/820ft at the outset. Unsuitable for beginners. Equipment as main walk. Access: 🚐 or 🚗 to Vatos (Glyfada bus); alight from the bus at the Vatos/Glyfada junction; park near the petrol station. Return as main walk — back to base, or back to your car at Vatos. Walk from the bus stop along to the tiny souvenir shop (closed at present) on the left, just before the petrol station. Here turn left, following the main walk from just after the 2h05min-point to the end.

Alternative walk: Gouvia — Scotini Pond — Ropa Plain — Vatos: 8.25km/5mi; 2h10min. Easy; stout shoes will suffice; access by 🚐 as main walk; return bus from Vatos (Glyfada bus). Follow the main walk to Vatos and continue on the main road past the petrol station. to the Pelekas/Glyfada junction. Catch the bus here, on the Corfu Town side of the road.

Cross the island from east to west and discover the diversity of Corfu's landscapes. Within a stone's throw of Gouvia's tourist haunts, you're in the countryside. Half an hour brings you to quiet rolling hills. You come upon a large pond full of terrapin and frogs, in an enchanting valley. Heading west, you cross the Ropa Plain — with a mere scattering of trees, it sits like an airfield, buried below hills. Ascending the slopes of Ag Georgios, the west coast unravels — in complete contrast to the east. Vivid green pines fleck the rocky sea-cliffs towering above some of the island's most beautiful beaches — the most spectacular being Mirtiotissa.

Start the walk at the bus stop in **Gouvia**: cross the road opposite FILIPA'S TAVERNA. Entering a country road, turn right (a left

Scotini Pond

leads to Danilia, the folklore village). At the third turning on the left, there is a sign, 'VILLA JASMIN' (**10min**): turn left here through the tourist hinterland. On crossing a low crest, you pass a large house on the left, surrounded by stone walls. Some 40m/yds past this house, take the second track turning off to the left. (A hedge of scrub hides this track until you're virtually on top of it.) A quarry scars the countryside ahead. Skirting a fenced-off field, descend into a gentle open valley. Five minutes off the road, you're overlooking **Scotini**, the pond shown on page 105. It's the only one up here that doesn't dry up.

A minute past the pond, head left at a junction and soon reach a ROAD (**40min**). Turn left and, three minutes along, take a side-road off to the right, passing a gauntlet of villas. A little over 10 minutes along, the road reverts to gravel. Two minutes later, ignore a track off to the right (where the main gravel road turns sharp left). A minute later ignore another faint track off to the right. Immediately after, the gravel road takes you past a house with a shrine in its garden.

Soon you're descending into the **Ropa Valley**. Just after ignoring a faint farm track off to the right, come to a junction, where a wide track cuts across in front of

you: follow it to the right. The Ropa Valley begins appearing in bits and pieces, over the trees. Gianades is the village visible midway up the Marmaro Hills, across the plain. Five minutes from the junction you join a track coming from the right. Keep left here (the surface becomes tarred almost immediately) and pass a few houses. A working quarry has eaten away half of the hillside on the left. Five minutes along the road, you emerge on the quarry road and turn right. Minutes down you're on the CORFU/LIAPADES ROAD (**1h35min**), where you turn right.

From here you cross the **Ropa Plain**. Some 40m/yds along the road, turn left on a farm track that strikes across the plain. In spring the grass is knee-high and full of flowers. *Attention:* this track ends at what *may* be a military installation; I may be wrong, but *don't take any photographs around here* or your film may be confiscated.

Continue to the right of the enclosure, on a fainter track. Twenty minutes along, at a T-junction, turn left. It's likely that you'll spot some birds now: crested larks, red storks, goldfinches, stonechats, whinchats. A ditch lined with cane accompanies you on the right. Some 150m/yds along, you cross this ditch on a animal path,

going over a STONE-PAVED FORD. Then start to cross the wide field ahead. Midway, you cross another ditch and see a third ditch ahead. This ditch curves around to the left. Follow it, keeping on the right-hand side of it. The golf course clubhouse is now visible over to the left, amidst trees. Vatos is the small village on the lower slopes of Mt Ag Georgios, also on the left. When you're directly facing the mountain, a gap

Mirtiotissa Beach (Picnic 15)

becomes visible in the hedge of cane up ahead. Continue alongside the ditch until it swings left, toward the golf course. Then pick up a path heading towards Mt Ag Georgios: it leads through the gap in the cane. You cross another couple of ditches; then, just after passing behind a fenced-off property, swing right, to reach the track ahead (about seven minutes from the ford crossing).

Turn left on the track and, in two minutes, come to the ERMONES ROAD, just where it enters **Vatos (2h05min)**. Turn left on the road. Two minutes along (less than 100m past a PETROL STATION), turn right on a narrow gravel track — the first one you come to. *(The Short walk begins here; the Alternative walk keeps ahead to the Pelekas/Glyfada junction.)* Almost straight away you're on a concrete lane. A couple of minutes uphill, the lane veers sharply left, in front of a house. Some 30m/yds beyond the house, go right on a path bordered by high fences. Following this old village path, you come out on a road just below Vatos, five minutes from the main road. Head right on this road and, in two minutes turn left uphill into the TOP PART OF **Vatos (2h20min)**. Continue straight through the village without turning off. In three minutes, turn right uphill on a tarred road, passing the village school. The tar reverts to gravel.

After a steady climb on the lower flanks of **Mt Ag Georgios**, you round the nose of the ridge and look down onto a beryl sea, as the hillside plummets to the rocks below. Further along the track, look back for the spectacular views along the hilly coastline. Fifteen minutes into the descent, the track forks. Descend to the left, pass-

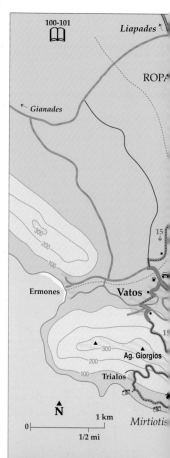

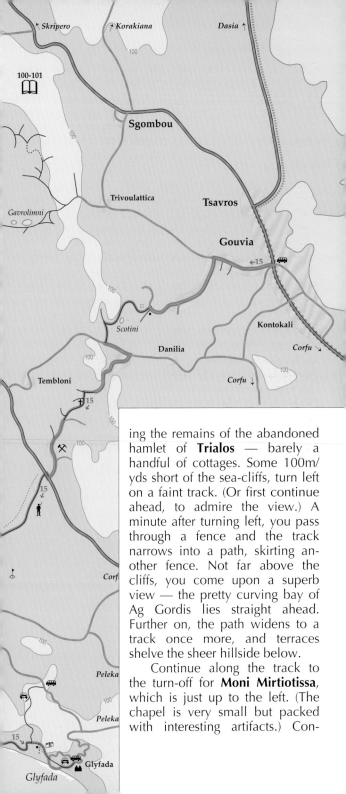

100-101

Skripero↗ ↗Korakiana Dasia ↑

100

Sgombou

Trivoulattica

Tsavros

Gavrolimni

Gouvia

←15

Scotini

Danilia

Kontokali

Corfu ↘

Tembloni

Corfu ↓

100

Temploni

Corf

Peleka

Peleka

15

Glyfada

Glyfada

ing the remains of the abandoned hamlet of **Trialos** — barely a handful of cottages. Some 100m/yds short of the sea-cliffs, turn left on a faint track. (Or first continue ahead, to admire the view.) A minute after turning left, you pass through a fence and the track narrows into a path, skirting another fence. Not far above the cliffs, you come upon a superb view — the pretty curving bay of Ag Gordis lies straight ahead. Further on, the path widens to a track once more, and terraces shelve the sheer hillside below.

Continue along the track to the turn-off for **Moni Mirtiotissa**, which is just up to the left. (The chapel is very small but packed with interesting artifacts.) Continuing along to the right here, the spectacular beach shown on pages 106-107 comes into sight, wrapped around the shore beneath towering pine-speckled cliffs. During the wet months, streamlets cascade down these rocky walls. The walled-in *moni,* almost hidden in trees, sits in solitude just out of sight of the beach. (A good thing perhaps, since Mirtiotissa is Corfu's well-known — although illegal — naturist beach.) So far, the inaccessibility of **Mirtiotissa Beach** (**3h20min**; Picnic 15) has deterred developers.

Heading on to Glyfada, follow the steep track from Mirtiotissa Beach. Close on 10 minutes uphill, just after an S-bend, turn right downhill on the first path you come to, towards a restaurant/bar set back in a dell of pines. Passing above the restaurant, keep straight on. Behind the toilets (to the left), take the path ahead, running between two fences *(Do not* descend to the right.) Crossing a small flat area, you overlook Glyfada — another stupendous setting below cliffs studded with beautiful, fluffy pines. But alas, a large hotel and apartment blocks have blighted the natural beauty of this spot. It's a popular beach with the local people.

Dropping down off this flat-topped clearing, you follow a watercourse and practically slide your way downhill. This descent is stony and very steep. Three minutes down you emerge at the back of a restaurant. From here, descend to the BEACH at **Glyfada** (**3h40min**). Head along the beach to the left for five minutes, then ascend a track to a large car park. Continue up the road for five minutes, to the junction above the hotel, where the bus turns around (**3h50min**).

16 ANO GAROUNA • MONI AG DEKA • WATERWORKS GARDEN • BENITSES

Distance/time: 7km/4.5mi; 2h25min

Grade: moderate, with an ascent of 280m/920ft on a clear but fairly overgrown path and a rather steep descent of 580m/1900ft

Equipment: walking boots, sunhat, sunglasses, suncream, long-sleeved shirt, long trousers (for protection from thorny scrub as well as the sun), cardigan, raingear, swimwear, picnic, water

How to get there: 🚌 to Ano Garouna; journey time 40min
To return: 🚌 from Benitses; journey time 30min

Short walk: Ano Garouna — Moni Ag Deka — Ano Garouna: 3.5km/2mi; 1h25min. Moderate ascent/descent of 280m/920ft (as above). Equipment and access as main walk; return on the same bus (or 🚗: park in the car park below Ano Garouna). Follow the main walk to the 45min-point and return the same way.

Mt Ag Deka, Corfu's second-highest peak (576m/1890ft), is a pint-sized mountain rising in the centre of the island. Atop it lies a shallow depression, the crater of an ancient volcano according to folklore. In the depression you find a rival for the Garden of Eden — an unkempt orchard boasting some 45 different varieties of fruits. Tucked away on the summit, behind creepered walls, sits the monastery *(moni)* of Pantokrator of Ag Deka, a cool, shady sanctuary. Both ascending and descending, you enjoy a magnificent

Gathering chestnuts in autumn at Moni Pantokrator of Ag Deka

panorama of the inland hills and vales edging out to the coasts, before they climb and tumble into the sea. Nearer the shore, you stumble onto an overgrown garden. This, surprisingly, is the waterworks, built over 150 years ago to furnish Corfu Town with water.

Start the walk at the BUS SHELTER/CAR PARKING AREA below **Ano Garouna**. Facing the village above, take a path ascending to the right, to the village centre. The path emerges just below a restaurant (currently closed). Continue up between the houses. Then take the first left (the alley to the right at this point leads past a couple of very old *cafeneions* and on to the village square). Keep left again almost immediately. At the next fork, keep right. This turn takes you out of the village. On coming to another fork (beside a large olive tree), go left. Three minutes out of the village, you pass above a stone farm shed and, five minutes further up, a track comes into sight not far above. Scramble up the hillside to this track and follow it to the left for 20m/yds. Then climb steps cut into the embankment on the right. In a couple of minutes you reach the track again, where you turn right uphill. When this track ends, continue on the overgrown path that leads off it.

Climbing, the views expand as far north as Panto-krator. A steady ascent brings you to a JUNCTION (**40min**) The village of Ag Deka (visited later in the walk) is down to the left; Moni Ag Deka is up to the right. Head right. Unaware, you enter the 'crater'. In a couple of minutes you're peering into the shady courtyard of **Moni Ag Deka** (**45min**), and you can quench your thirst at the well. The chapel is unlocked; the monks' quarters are now used only for storage, or when a local festivity takes grip of the site.

Return to the junction below the *moni* and keep straight on (right) for the village of Ag Deka. Ten minutes downhill you pass a prominent rock — an excellent viewpoint. You look straight down onto the lagoon near the airport. Villages encircled by olive groves lie scattered amidst the hills. The prominent white building down to the right is the Achilleion Palace. Ten minutes beyond the viewpoint, ignore two forks off to the right, a minute apart. Three minutes later, the main path forks. This time, head right, soon passing to the right of a concrete shed. Continuing straight on, you find yourself walking alongside a fat water pipe. The path widens into a faint track. Coming

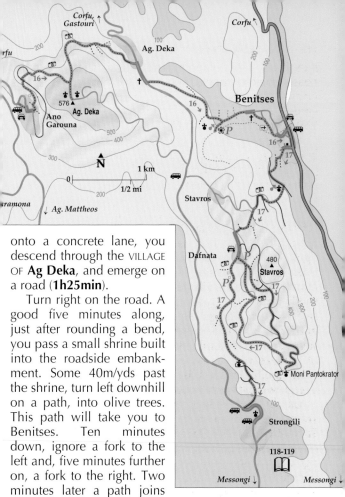

Corfu,
Gastouri

Corfu

rfu

Ag. Deka

16→

Benitses

576▲
Ag. Deka

16↓

Ano
Garouna

16→

17

N

1 km

0

1/2 mi

Stavros

ramona ↓ Ag. Mattheos

Dafnata

17

480 ▲
Stavros

17

17↓

17↓

←17

Moni Pantokrator

17↓

Strongili

118-119

Messongi ↓

Messongi ↓

onto a concrete lane, you descend through the VILLAGE OF **Ag Deka**, and emerge on a road (**1h25min**).

Turn right on the road. A good five minutes along, just after rounding a bend, you pass a small shrine built into the roadside embankment. Some 40m/yds past the shrine, turn left downhill on a path, into olive trees. This path will take you to Benitses. Ten minutes down, ignore a fork to the left and, five minutes further on, a fork to the right. Two minutes later a path joins from the left. On coming to a T-junction, turn right. In two minutes you're at the WATERWORKS GARDEN (**2h**; Picnic 16). A stream runs down the valley floor, which is a lush exuberant tangle of vegetation. This pretty spot is like a wild garden.

Return to the T-junction and now keep straight on, through orchards and vegetable gardens. A causeway takes you to the end of a road. Follow the road for a minute, then descend steps alongside a garish shrine. Follow the path below the shrine, bearing left into the trees. The path emerges on the road to the water treatment plant. Pick up your continuing path opposite its gateway, and head left. Passing the cemetery, you join a narrow road which takes you straight to the main square at **Benitses** (**2h25min**). You can take any bus (green or blue) on the sea side of the main road.

17 BENITSES • DAFNATA • STRONGILI

See map page 113 **Distance/time:** 10km/6.25mi; 3h50min

Grade: strenuous, with an ascent of 400m/1300ft and descent of 400m/1300ft (dangerous if wet)

Equipment: walking boots or stout shoes with grip and ankle support, sunhat, sunglasses, suncream, long-sleeved shirt, long trousers, cardigan, raingear, swimwear, picnic, water

How to get there: 🚌 to Benitses; journey time 30min
To return: 🚌 from Strongili; journey time 1h

Alternative walk: Benitses — Dafnata — Moni Pantokrator — Benitses: 9.5km/6mi; 3h35min. Grade, equipment and access as main walk; return on the same bus (or 🚗 to/from Benitses — arrive early, to find a parking place!). Follow the main walk to Moni Pantokrator, then return to Dafnata and take your outgoing path back to Benitses.

Winding up through cypresses and olive groves, you climb to the hillside village of Dafnata, trailing superb coastal scenery behind you. The village sits high and fast on table-topped Mt Stavros. Across the mountain stands the little chapel of Pantokrator.

Start the walk at **Benitses**: head south along the main road. Just after passing the Hotel Potamaki on the right, turn right on a road. (A yellow dot marks this turn-off.) On coming to a T-junction running parallel with a ditch (**2min**), turn left. Then, 30m/yds along, go left on a path. Yellow dots reappear. Barely a minute along the path, just after a fenced-off olive grove, ascend steps to the right. At the top of the the steps the path swings left. At another junction (by an electricity pole), turn right up a cobbled path, as indicated by a yellow arrow. Ignore a turn-off to the right; remain on the cobbled path, to round the hillside above Benitses. Three minutes past the turn-off, a fence is on your left. The way fades as you climb: be sure to keep to the right of the olive grove.

On meeting a TRACK (**30min**), turn left. Five minutes along the track, turn right on the drive up to a chapel, where a refreshing, cool spring in the shade of an enormous oak tree awaits you. Moving on, follow the path running below the chapel courtyard, heading round the hillside and crossing a dry stream bed. Two minutes along, the path climbs to a track (just at the point where the track ends). Here head right on a path that continues off the track and along the hillside. Two minutes further on, you rejoin the track and follow it to the right. Rounding a bend, there is a lovely view down over Benitses and along the coast to Corfu Town.

A little over five minutes uphill (one minute after the track becomes tarred and just at the start of an olive grove), turn left uphill on a footpath, climbing into tall

114

scruffy cypress trees. Five minutes uphill, *watch for a fork* and head right uphill on a faint zigzag path. At the T-junction a few minutes up, go right. This turn brings you to another junction just below the road: keep left here, and go left again on the road. Five minutes uphill, the road ends in **Dafnata**; continue straight along an alley, to a small square with a tree (**1h15min**).

As soon as you enter the square, take the first path left uphill (at the *top* of the square). Then turn right

On the slopes of Mt Stavros, between Moni Pantokrator and Dafnata

immediately, making your way behind the houses, to begin the ascent of Mt Stavros. Soon there is a superb outlook across the centre of the island (one setting for Picnic 17). Three minutes along the path, ignore a turn-off to the right (your return route). Just past the turn-off, ignore a fork to the left. Your destination is the hilltop over to the right. Ignore another, faint fork to the left barely two minutes further on. Cross a track below a fenced-off area, to rejoin the path rounding the hillside. When you reach a track, turn right along it and follow it across the shoulder of **Mt Stavros**, ignoring a track off to the left and, five minutes later, a track off to the right.

Moni Pantokrator (**2h**) stands on a rocky outcrop at the end of the track, hanging out over the Messongi Valley. Inside the chapel are some barely-discernible frescoes and an excellent canvas. Before heading on, get your bearings. Facing the track, look over to the left, to see you return route below, running along the slopes of Mt Stavros. Then head back up the track for 25m/yds and take a path descending to the left (beside a large rock). Ignore a fork off left two minutes down. Circling the mountainside, you catch sight of Strongili below. Half an hour from the chapel, ignore a faint turn-off to the left. (It's a short-cut to the Strongili path below, but is overgrown.) Coming into olive groves again, keep uphill to the right, soon rejoining your outgoing path, where you turn left. Two minutes down, you're back at the square in **Dafnata** (**2h35min**).

Descending to Strongili, head left from the bottom of the square, following a yellow arrow. A stony path takes you down into cypresses (another setting for Picnic 17). Keep to the main path, passing some corrugated iron sheds on your right. At this stage, ignore any paths off to the right. About 10 minutes from the square, above a roofless stone building, keep left at a fork. At the next fork, five minutes later, go right. Shortly afterwards, Strongili reappears. Five minutes from the last fork, you find yourself alongside a chapel. Heading behind it, meet a track and turn left. The track forks immediately: keep right downhill. In five minutes, when the track forks again, go right and, metres/yards downhill, go left on a path (yellow arrow on a tree). Passing a farm shed on the right, pick up a faint track, which brings you down to the Strongili road (**3h45min**). Flag down a bus here or, better, turn left into **Strongili** (**3h50min**), where there is a choice of cafés as well as a bus stop.

18 MESSONGI • AG DIMITRIOS • HLOMOS • KOUSPADES • KORAKADES • PETRETI • PERIVOLION

See also photograph page 40

Distance/time: 14.5km/9mi; 3h35min

Grade: easy to moderate, with a steep ascent of 300m/1000ft at the start

Equipment: stout shoes, sunhat, sunglasses, suncream, long-sleeved shirt, long trousers, raingear, swimwear, picnic, water

How to get there: 🚌 to Messongi (or Kavos bus to Messongi); journey time 45min; or 🚗 to Messongi; park along the seafront, inside the village, at the side of the main south road.

To return: 🚌 from Perivolion; journey time 1h05min, back to Corfu Town, or to your car at Messongi

This walk may not appeal to everyone, because at least half of it is along asphalt roads. But outside peak season they carry only a trickle of traffic. Charming villages and hamlets lie on route; each has its own personality. They adorn ridges, step hillsides, and dribble down slopes to the sea. You wind your way around the sylvan, seaward slopes, through olive groves and down lanes of cypress trees. Seascapes ebb and flow.

Start out at the bus stop/turnaround in **Messongi**. Walk back the way the bus came into the village and, at the T-junction (**2min**), turn left towards Ag Dimitrios. Follow the road uphill past Kato Spilion, a small village on a side-road off to the right. On arriving at the village of **Ag Dimitrios** (**55min**), the road swings left to Hlomos. But, before heading along it, continue up to the right for a minute — to enjoy a superb panorama encompassing the central mountains, the gulf and the Pantokrator hills. Returning to the Hlomos road, follow it for a little over 1km, then take first turn-off to the left — up to the top of this cascading village. Two minutes uphill, turn right along a lane; it curves to the left, passing below the church.

From the CHURCH at **Hlomos** (**1h20min**; Picnic 18a) there are fine views along the northern coastline to Mt Pantokrator, and south to the tip of the island. The village steps the hillside below.

Leaving the church, head back along the lane, then take the first

Hlomos

117

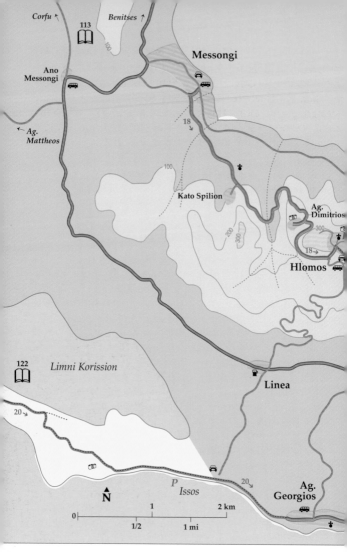

alley off left, following a sign for TAVERNA SIRTAKI. Old houses flank the alley. A minute down, either head right to the taverna or turn left and then go right immediately, to descend to the village square, a minute below. On reaching the narrow square, continue straight downhill. (Coming from the taverna, this is the first right turn out of the square.)

Half a minute down from the square, descend steps to the right, then continue along the path, down into a gully. The way heads along the side of a steep embankment. Ten minutes downhill, you encounter two forks, one after the other: keep right at both of them. Red arrows and dots mark this part of the trail. A minute later, ignore a path off to the right. Soon after, you meet a track (just where it veers off to the left). Continue straight ahead along this track. Just after a fork off to the right, come to a junction and again continue straight ahead, ignoring the fork to the left.

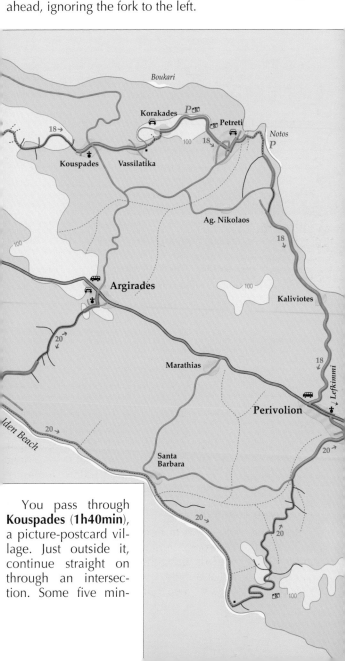

You pass through **Kouspades** (**1h40min**), a picture-postcard village. Just outside it, continue straight on through an intersection. Some five minutes later, pass through **Vassilatika**. A few minutes later, just beyond a factory, leave the road and ascend a path to the right.

Keep straight on (right) at the junction three minutes uphill, to come into **Korakades**, where you turn right along the village lane. An air of abandon hangs over this farming settlement. Soon the lane veers sharp left. Descending past derelict houses (Picnic 18b), you wind your way down the hillside, with tremendous views through the trees on the left over to the hills of Epirus.

A good 10 minutes down, meet a road on the outskirts of the small fishing village of **Petreti**. Cross the road and continue downhill on a road more or less opposite. A minute later, you cross the road again. At the bottom of the road, bear left. Then, 100m/yds along, take the road forking off right, down to a mud-flat beach (**2h30min**). Now continue to the right, along the seafront. After crossing a couple of reedy streams, head right, through a gap in a stone wall, to ascend the crest of a low hill. Beyond the pretty cove of **Notos** (Picnic 18c), climb a concrete lane, cross another crest, and continue along a dirt track.

Within 10 minutes, at a T-junction, turn left along the road and follow it for 45 minutes, to **Perivolion** (**3h35min**). The BUS STOP is in front of the cafés and bars, just to the right of the T-junction.

The canal at the Korission Lagoon (the 1h45min-point in Walk 20), with Mt Ag Mattheos (Walk 19) rising in the background

19 MT AG MATTHEOS

Photograph page 24 (photographs of Mt Ag Mattheos page 15 and opposite)

Distance/time: 6km/3.75mi; 2h20min

Grade: strenuous, with an ascent of 300m/1000ft on a track and a descent of 300m/1000ft on a rocky path and track

Equipment: walking boots, sunhat, sunglasses, suncream, long-sleeved shirt, long trousers, raingear, picnic, plenty of water

How to get there and return: 🚌 to/from Ag Mattheos village; journey time 50min, or 🚗: park on the main road south of the village, near the bakery where the mountain track begins.

The panoramic view over the south of the island from Mt Ag Mattheos is well worth the climb. It's best done in the late afternoon, when it's cooler and the light is softer. While the track that you follow on the ascent is wide and ugly, scarring the whole mountainside, the descent path through the kermes oak wood (one of the few left on the island), is ample compensation.

Start the walk in the village of **Ag Mattheos**, outside the row of cafés and restaurants on the main road. Follow the main road south for a little over five minutes. Near the end of the village, immediately past a bakery on the right, turn right up a lane. (It's unmissable: as soon as you turn off you'll spot a garden with gnomes — Snow White and the Seven Dwarfs!) Ignore the turn-off to the right soon afterwards. Soon concrete comes underfoot, then gravel. Two more tracks join from the right within the first 10 minutes: continue straight uphill. At the next fork, go right (to the left is the original mountain track, now mostly bulldozed away).

Ascending, there is a good outlook over the thickly-wooded Messongi basin below. Higher up, you enjoy a bird's-eye view over the village of Ag Mattheos, then Messongi Bay. The east coast slowly unravels and, on a bend, you look out over the Korission Lagoon (**1h**). Soon the kermes oak wood closes in around you.

Just below the summit you reach **Moni Pantokrator (1h25min)**. Standing below the compound, pick up the path that climbs to the left of the *moni* and to a superb lookout point a couple of minutes further up. From the shelter of a fern-leaf hut, you can enjoy the view along the east coast, with its crystal-clear sea. A minute later you're on the SUMMIT OF **Mt Ag Mattheos (1h30min)**. From here the view stretches to both sides of the island. In October the rocky hilltop is a mass of cyclamen and crocuses, and tiny goldcrests and redstarts flit about the wood, while the occasional buzzard circles overhead.

121

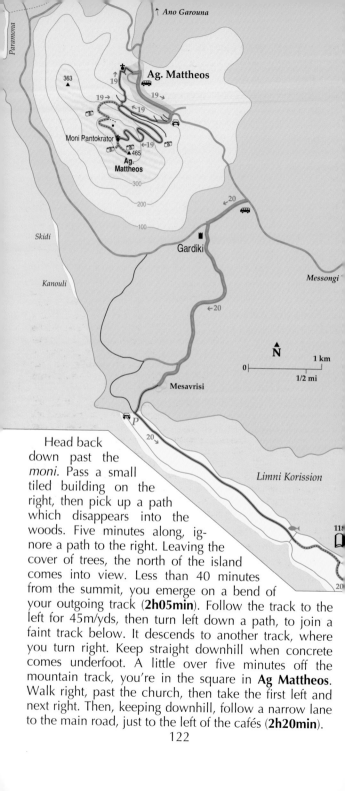

↑ *Ano Garouna*

Paramona

Ag. Mattheos

363 ▲

19

19→

←19

19→

Moni Pantokrator

←19

▲465

Ag. Mattheos

←20

Skidi

Gardiki

Kanouli

Messongi

←20

N

0 —————————— 1 km
—————————— 1/2 mi

Mesavrisi

P

20→

Limni Korission

118

20

Head back down past the *moni*. Pass a small tiled building on the right, then pick up a path which disappears into the woods. Five minutes along, ignore a path to the right. Leaving the cover of trees, the north of the island comes into view. Less than 40 minutes from the summit, you emerge on a bend of your outgoing track (**2h05min**). Follow the track to the left for 45m/yds, then turn left down a path, to join a faint track below. It descends to another track, where you turn right. Keep straight downhill when concrete comes underfoot. A little over five minutes off the mountain track, you're in the square in **Ag Mattheos**. Walk right, past the church, then take the first left and next right. Then, keeping downhill, follow a narrow lane to the main road, just to the left of the cafés (**2h20min**).

20 GARDIKI CASTLE • KORISSION LAGOON • AG GEORGIOS • GOLDEN BEACH • PERIVOLION

Map begins opposite, ends on pages 118-119; see photographs pages 15, 40, 120

Distance/time: 22.5km/14mi; 6h10min

Grade: easy; all along a beach ... but plodding over sand is tiring. Steep climb of 100m/330ft to reach Perivolion.

Equipment: as little as possible! Light trainers for reaching and leaving beaches (and the odd stretch of rock), sunhat, sunglasses, high-protection suncream, swimwear, picnic, plenty of water

How to get there: 🚌 to the Gardiki turn-off (Ag Mattheos bus); journey time 45min. Or 🚌 or 🚗 to Messongi (park on the main road, just outside the centre of Messongi) and taxi to 'Lake' Korission.* (Motorists who just want a stroll can park down by the lagoon.)
To return: 🚌 from Perivolion — back to Corfu Town; journey time 1h05min, or back to your 🚗 at Messongi or Ano Messongi

Short walks

1 Gardiki Castle — Ag Georgios — Argirades: 15km/9.5mi; 4h. Easy; equipment and access as main walk; return by bus from Argirades (back to Corfu Town or back to your car). Follow the main walk to Golden Beach, then walk along the country road to Argirades (signposted five minutes past the church in Ag Georgios, just before Golden Beach; see map on pages 118-119). On entering Argirades, keep straight ahead to the church square. Then turn left and, when you reach the main road, follow it uphill for 100m/yds. The bus stops in front of the first large olive tree on the right.

2 Argirades — Golden Beach — Perivolion: 12km/7.5mi; 3h45min. Grade and equipment as main walk. Access: Kavos 🚌 or 🚗 to Argirades (park at the side of the main road, near the turn-off for Kouspades and Petreti). Start out at the turn-off for Kouspades and Petreti. Take the lane diagonally opposite, heading into the church square in Argirades. Beyond the church go right. Ignore a fork off to the right, and remain on this small country road all the way to Golden Beach (see map on pages 118-119). Join the main walk at the 3h10min-point and follow it to the end. Return as the main walk — back to Corfu Town, or back to your car at Argirades.

Almost all of this walk extends along the seashore — a seemingly-endless sandy beach. 'Lake' Korission, where you first meet the sea, is a shallow lagoon bordered by a causeway of sand dunes. Traipsing across these dunes you pass through an enchanting thicket of holly oak, an pretty interlude before you come upon the *real* dunes — billows of golden sand splashed with silver-green clumps of juniper. Ag Georgios, off to a bad start in its rush to meet tourist demands, briefly disrupts the landscape as you cut off a corner of rocky coastline to rejoin the shore. The dunes now behind you, you paddle along below sandstone banks that

*Or begin at Ano Messongi and walk along the busy country road to the Gardiki turn-off (40min), thus dispensing with a taxi.

soon grow into cliffs, and you return to deserted beaches and the sound of the sea.

The walk starts at the TURN-OFF to **Gardiki Castle**. Follow the road to the CASTLE (**10min**), keeping left at the fork just before it. Just under 20 minutes later, bear left on the tarred road to **Mesavrisi**. Reaching the beach and the causeway of dunes at the **Korission Lagoon** (**50min**), continue to the left (Picnic 20a).

When you reach the FISH FARM and the CANAL joining the so-called 'lake' to the sea (**1h45min**), cross the canal near the shed shown on page 120, then follow the sandy path into scrub (now referring to the map on pages 118-119). The path veers towards the lagoon and follows it for five minutes. Then, without warning, it swings right, back into the scrub (take care not to continue along the side of the lagoon). Soon a disused track comes underfoot. Emerging from the scrub, climb over the dunes, meandering through clumps of juniper and overlooking a landscape very unlike the olive-clad hills of the rest of Corfu: a lagoon trimmed in sedge and a countryside sparingly sprinkled with cottages.

On coming to the SEA (**2h20min**), head left towards Ag Georgios, passing **Issos Beach** (Picnic 20b). Follow the road through **Ag Georgios** then, just past the sign-posted turn-off to Argirades, descend to **Golden Beach** (**3h10min**). *(Short walk 1 leaves via the Argirades turn-off, and Short walk 2 joins here.)* Head left along the beach, sometimes scrambling over rocks. After 50 minutes you pass the holiday village of **Santa Barbara** (**4h**). Further along this relatively-deserted coast, you round a rocky PROMONTORY (**4h45min**), a sheltered swimming spot with a flotilla of dinghies. Head over to the small brick building at the back of this beach and take the track that passes in front of it, to leave the beach. A couple of minutes along, you join two more tracks ascending from the beach. Climbing, you have a beautiful view of a near-deserted beach further along the coast. A steep climb brings you up to a JUNCTION (**5h 15min**). Go left and then immediately right downhill.

Less than 20 minutes down, ignore side-tracks, first to the right, then left, then right again. Join the SANTA BARBARA ROAD, and head right. Entering **Perivolion**, keep left (but *not* sharp left) at a junction. At the junction in front of the church belfry, go left again on the main road. The BUS STOP (**6h10min**) lies a couple of minutes along, in front of the cafés on the right.

21 KAVOS • MONI PANAGIA • ARKOUDILLAS BEACH • KANULA BEACH • PALEOCHORI

See also photograph page 4   **Distance/time:** 10km/6.2mi; 3h15min

Grade: moderate, with ascents/descents of about 200m/650ft. Care is needed occasionally, clambering over rocks.

Equipment: walking boots or stout shoes, sunhat, sunglasses, suncream, long-sleeved shirt, long trousers, raingear, swimwear, picnic, plenty of water

How to get there: 🚌 to Kavos; journey time 1h45min
To return: 🚌 from Paleochori (recheck departure time, as these bus times depend on school holidays); journey time 1h50min.

Short walk: Kavos — Moni Panagia — Arkoudillas Beach — Kavos: 8km/5mi; 2h20min. Easy ascents/descents of 100m/330ft; equipment and access as main walk; return on the same bus. Or 🚗 to/from Kavos: motorists should continue through the village and park at the side of the track to the monastery (see map), saving a total of 15min. Equipment and access as above. Follow the main walk to Arkoudillas Beach, then return on the beach track, keeping right uphill at the fork. A little over five minutes up, rejoin your outward track to the monastery, and turn left for Kavos. *Strongly recommended for beginners.*

At the tip of the island, in a neighbourhood of holly oaks and cypresses, lie the remains of a fortified monastery — Moni Panagia Arkoudillas. This romantic ruin sits back just out of sight of the beautifully-eroded cliffs of Cape Asprokavos. The multitude of names scrawled on the monastery walls indicates that this is probably the most walked (or cycled) track on Corfu. For the locals however, the only interest this point holds

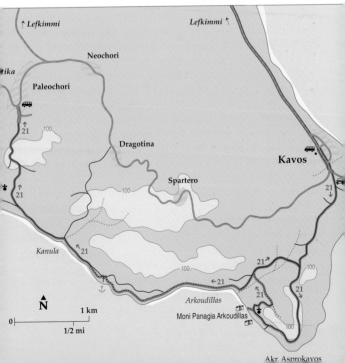

Arkoudillas Beach

is for shooting. Don't expect to see any birds around.

Get off the bus at the last stop in **Kavos**. **Start out** by keeping ahead on the main road, passing the MEDICAL CENTRE (which should be on your right when you alight from the bus.) At the JUNCTION (**5min**), turn right. A minute later cross a bridge, then follow the road to the left. Barely one minute further on, leave the road and turn right on a gravel TRACK SIGNPOSTED FOR MONI PANAGIA. This broad track takes you straight to the monastery. In the first few minutes ignore turn-offs to the left then the right. And within the following 10 minutes ignore two more tracks off to the right. *(The Short walk will return later along the second track.)*

Pass a DUMP beside the track (**45min**); at the fork five minutes later, keep right. Cypress trees line the track and, further along, you're in the shade of a pretty oak wood, one of the few surviving on the island. Vines hang from the trees. Approaching the monastery, the track runs along the clifftops, which are hidden by vegetation. There are superb views along the dazzling white cliffs. (If you scramble up to the edge of the cliff for a better view, do so with the utmost care! These cliffs crumble away easily.)

Five minutes from the fork, **Moni Panagia** (**55min**) suddenly appears, in a clump of cypress trees below the track. Inside the walls are two chapels: one belongs to the original monastery and is now only a shell; the other, more recent but rather dilapidated, remains open and is still in use. Remains of stairways and walls add to the charm of the site, the more so in spring and autumn when speckled with wild flowers. Take the path on the far side of the track, heading off into the trees. It's overgrown and involves a lot of bending and ducking, but this short foray only takes two minutes. It takes you along the edge of the cliff, revealing a spectacular view over Arkoudillas Beach, which you will visit later.

Return to the monastery and follow the track as it winds down through this enchanting forest, where the olive groves are being swallowed up by kermes oaks.

Minutes downhill, the track ends at a T-junction with a path. Head left for the beach. The path disappears into scrub: push and shove your way through — the path is always clear. Five minutes down the path, cross a muddy stream, then scramble up through scrub to a WIDE DIRT TRACK (**1h25min**). Follow the track down to the left and, after a few metres/yards, keep left at the fork. Minutes later you're standing on deserted **Arkoudillas Beach** (**1h30min**). *(From here the Short walk returns up the track, keeping straight uphill at the fork.)*

The main walk continues along the broad sweep of the bay, towards the cape. Amongst the seashore rocks, you come across rock samphire *(Crithmum maritimum)*, a strange-smelling plant with blue-to-green fleshy leaves. Around 25 minutes along the beach, you pass below a track, but remain along the shoreline. Skirting a rocky headland, soon come to a makeshift marina (**Kanula Bay**) with a number of dinghies. A brief clamber over large boulders is necessary here, to climb up to a GRAVEL ROAD (**2h15min**).

Once on the road, you can either follow it behind **Kanula Beach** or walk along the shore. Some 35 minutes along the beach (about midway), you join another gravel road, to climb inland towards Paleochori, passing a chapel en route. Remain on the widest road all the way into **Paleochori** (**3h15min**), then follow the road as it curves to the left downhill, to the junction where you catch the bus.

Moni Panagia Arkoudillas. The Short walk is recommended for everyone, and would round off Car tour 4 perfectly.

BUS TIMETABLES

Note that these timetables were valid during the peak season at press date. On either side of summer they may vary, cuts being made in mid-September and October (when there may be only a skeleton service until May). It is possible that there are more frequent services than those shown here, which were taken from *printed timetables*. It is always worth checking to see if more buses are running. Use these timetables as a guide to *frequency* of services *only*; no doubt further changes will be made. *For all buses except those with a fairly frequent service, you must check and recheck both departure and return times* **at the bus station**.

The timetables on the following pages make reference to two bus stations. 'Station 1' is the terminal at the front of San Rocco Square/ Platia Georgiou Theotoki (buses for the nearby resorts both north and south of Corfu Town, ie Dasia, Potamos, Benitses, etc); 'Station 2' is the New Fortress Square station, near the old port. These buses go to all other destinations on the island. Both stations have timetables posted on site. Station 2 has a printed giveaway timetable as well, but it only covers the main tourist centres. (Timetables are also printed in tourist newspapers and leaflets.) When catching a bus from Station 2, always arrive 15 minutes early; it will take you that long to find your bus — the station is fairly chaotic, especially in high season. Moreover the bus conductors and drivers at Station 2 seem to change daily, so they are not always a reliable source of information! Remember this, when you go to confirm and reconfirm times for your return bus: the staff very often cannot remember and so they make a guess — and get it wrong! Be sure to recheck return times before setting out *with the bus conductor/driver with whom you make the outward journey*. (There is a third station in Corfu Town, the 'Esplanade' Station; this is for suburban buses only.)

Acharavi (Station 2). See Timetable 9
Achilleion (Bus No 10, Station 1). Departs 07.00, 10.00, 12.00, 14.15, 17.00, 20.00 (Mon-Fri); departs 09.00, 12.00, 17.00, 20.00 (Sat/ Sun/holidays). Returns 15 minutes later
Afionas (Station 2). See Timetable 10
Afra (Bus No 8, Station 1). Departs 06.00, 07.00, 09.00, 11.00, 14.15, 17.00, 19.00, 21.00 (Mon-Fri); departs 08.00, 13.00, 16.00, 18.00, 20.00 (Sat/Sun/holidays). Returns 30 minutes later
Ag Georgios Beach (Station 2). See Timetable 7
Ag Gordis (Station 2). See Timetable 4
Ag Ioannis (Station 2). See Timetable 5
Ag Martinos (Station 2). Departs 05.30, 13.30 (Mon-Sat only). Returns 06.50, 14.50 (Mon-Sat only). Journey time 1h20min
Ag Mattheos (Station 2). Departs 05.15, 06.15, 07.00, 12.00, 13.00, 14.00, 16.30 (Mon-Sat); departs 09.15, 16.00 (Sun/holidays). Returns 06.15, 07.15, 08.00, 13.00, 15.30, 17.30 (Mon-Sat); returns 16.00 (Sun/ holidays). Journey time 45min
Ag Pandelimonas (Station 2). Departs 05.30, 14.00 (Mon-Sat only). Returns 07.00, 15.30 (Mon-Sat only). Journey time 1h30min
Ag Stefanos (at Cape Ag Stefanos) (Station 2). See Timetable 8
Ag Stefanos (near Kouloura) (Station 2). See Timetable 11
Alepou (Bus No 8, Station 1). Departs 09.20 (Mon-Fri). Returns 09.30
Ano Garouna (Station 2). Departs 05.00, 06.30, 12.30, 15.15 (Mon-Sat only). Returns 06.15, 07,10, 13.10, 15.55 (Mon-Sat only). Journey time 40min
Argirades (Station 2). See Timetables 2 and 7

Arilas (Station 2). See Timetable 10

Arkadades (Station 2). See Timetable 8

Armenades (Station 2). Departs 06.30, 13.30 (Mon-Sat only). Returns 07.45, 14.45 (Mon-Sat only). Journey time 1h05min

Avliotes (Station 2). See Timetable 8

Benitses (Bus No 6, Station 2). Departs 07.00, 08.00, 09.30, 10.30, 11.30, 13.15, 14.15, 16.00, 17.00, 19.00, 20.00, 21.30 (Mon-Fri); departs 08.30, 10.30, 12.30, 16.30, 18.30, 20.30 (Sat/Sun/hols). Returns 30mins later.

Dasia (Bus No 7, Station 1). Departs from 07.00 to 22.00 every half hour (daily). Returns 30 minutes later.

Doukades turn-off (Station 2). See Timetable 1; times approximately as Paleokastritsa

Episkepsis (Station 2). Departs 05.30, 14.00 (Mon-Sat only). Returns 07.15, 15.45 (Mon-Sat only). Journey time 1h15min

Ermones (Station 2). See Timetable 6

Gastouri (Bus No 10, Station 1). As Archilleion; returns 15 minutes later

Gianades (Station 2). Departs 05.00, 06.30, 14.30 (Mon-Sat only). Returns 05.35, 07.05, 15.00 (Mon Sat only). Journey time 35min

Glyfada (Station 2). See Timetable 5

Gouvia (Station 1). As Dasia

Hlomos (Station 2). Departs 05.45, 14.30 (Mon-Sat only). Returns 06.45, 15.30 (Mon-Sat only). Journey time 1h

Ipsos (Station 2). See Timetable 12

Kalami turn-off (Station 2). See Timetable 11

Kanoni (Bus No 2, Esplanade). Departs daily from 07.30 to 20.30 every 30 minutes; return journeys every 30 minutes

Karoussades (Station 2). Departs 06.00, 09.00, 14.00 (Mon-Sat only). Returns 07.10, 10.10, 15.10 (Mon-Sat only). Journey time 1h10min

Kassiopi (Station 2). See Timetables 11, 13

Kastellani (Station 2). See Timetable 4.

Kavadades/Magoulades junction (Station 2). See Timetable 10; times as Magoulades

Kavos (Station 2). See Timetable 2

Khoroepiskopi (Station 2). See Timetable 9

Kontokali (Bus No 7, Station 1). As Dasia

Korakades (Station 2). Departs 05.30, 14.00 (Mon-Sat only). Returns 06.30, 15.00 (Mon-Sat only). Journey time 1h

Korakiana (Station 2). Departs 06.15, 16.00 (Mon-Sat); departs 09.30, 19.30 (Sun/holidays). Returns 06.50, 16.35 (Mon-Sat); returns 10.05, 20.05 (Sun/holidays). Journey time 35min

Krini (Station 2). Departs 07.00, 14.50 (Mon-Sat only). Returns 07.05, 15.30 (Mon-Sat only). Journey time 1h

Lafki (Station 2). Departs 04.45, 14.00 (Mon-Sat only). Returns 06.55, 16.10 (Mon-Sat only). Journey time 2h10min

Lefkimmi (Station 2). See Timetable 2

Liapades (Station 2). Departs 05.00, 06.00, 14.00 (Mon-Sat only). Returns 05.35, 06.35, 14.35 (Mon-Sat only). Journey time 35min

Loutses (Station 2). See Timetable 11

Magoulades (Station 2). See Timetable 10. Departures also from Station 3 (via Armenades) at 06.30, 13.30. Returns 07.35, 15.00 (Mon-Sat only). Journey time 1h05min

Messongi (Station 2). See Timetables 2, 3

Nimfes (Station 2). Departs 05.30, 14.00 (Mon-Sat only). Returns 06.20, 14.50 (Mon-Sat only). Journey time 50min

Nissaki (Station 2). See Timetable 11

Paleochori (Station 2). Scheduling variable; check times at station

Paleokastritsa (Station 2). See Timetable 1

Perama (Bus No 6, Station 1). As No 6 Bus to Benitses (see above)

Perithia (Station 2). See Timetable 11

Perivolion (Station 2). See Timetable 2

Peroulades (Station 2). See Timetable 8

Porta (Station 2). Departs 05.45, 13.30 (Mon-Sat only). Returns 06.55, 14.40 (Mon-Sat only). Journey time 1h10min

Prinilas (Station 2). Departs 06.15, 13.30 (Mon-Sat only). Returns 07.15, 14.30 (Mon-Sat only). Journey time 1h

Pyrgi (Station 2). See Timetable 12

Roda (Station 2). See Timetables 9, 13

Sfakera (Station 2). Roda bus; see Timetable 9; times approximately as for Roda

Sgombou (Station 2). See Timetable 1; times approximately as for Tsavros

Sidari (Station 2). See Timetables 8, 13

Sinarades (Station 2). See Timetable 4

Sokraki (Station 2). Departs 04.45, 14.00 (Mon-Sat only). Returns 07.40, 16.55 (Mon-Sat only). Journey time 1h25min

Spartilas (Station 2). Departs 05.30, 14.00 (Mon-Sat only). Returns 08.00, 16.30 (Mon-Sat only). Journey time 40min

Stavros (Station 2). As Strongili

Strinilas (Station 2). See Lafki bus. Journey time approx. 1h30min

Strongili (Station 2). Departs 05.15, 06.15, 08.30, 12.30, 14.30, 17.00, 19.30 (Mon-Sat); departs 09.15 (Sun/holidays). Returns 06.15, 07.15, 09.30, 13.30, 15.30, 18.00, 20.30 (Mon-Sat); returns 16.00 (Sun/holidays). Journey time 1h

Tembloni (Bus No 4, Station 1). Departs 06.45, 14.30 (Mon-Fri only). Returns 07.00, 14.45 (Mon-Fri only).

Troumpeta (Station 2). See Timetable 9

Tsavros (Station 2). See Timetable 1

Variapatades (Station 2). Departs 05.30, 07.00, 14.30 (Mon-Sat only). Returns 06.05, 07.35, 15.05 (Mon-Sat only). Journey time 35min

Vassili (Bus No 3, Station 1). Departs daily 07.30 to 20.30 every 30 minutes. Return journeys every 30 minutes

Vatos (Station 2). See Timetable 5

Vitalades (Station 2). Departs 05.45 (Mon-Sat only). Returns 07.15 (Mon-Sat only). Journey time 1h10min

1 Corfu • Tsavros • Paleokastritsa (also Sgombou, Doukades turn-off)

Monday to Saturday			Sundays and holidays		
Corfu	Tsavros	Paleokastritsa	Corfu	Tsavros	Paleokastritsa
08.30	08.50	09.05	09.00	09.20	09.35
09.00	09.20	09.45	10.30	10.50	11.05
10.30	10.50	11.05	12.00	12.20	12.35
12.00	12.20	12.35	16.00	16.20	16.35
14.00	14.20	14.45	18.00	18.20	18.35
16.00	16.20	16.45			
18.00	18.20	18.45			

RETURN BUSES

Monday to Saturday			Sundays and holidays		
Paleokastritsa	Tsavros	Corfu	Paleokastritsa	Tsavros	Corfu
09.15	09.30	09.50	09.45	10.00	10.20
09.45	10.00	10.20	11.15	11.30	11.50
11.15	11.30	11.20	12.45	13.00	13.20

Paleokastritsa	Tsavros	Corfu	Paleokastritsa	Tsavros	Corfu
12.45	12.30	12.50	16.45	17.00	17.20
15.00	15.15	15.35	18.45	19.00	19.20
16.45	17.00	17.20			
18.45	19.00	19.20			

2 Corfu • Messongi • Argirades • Perivolion • Lefkimmi • Kavos

		Daily			
Corfu	Messongi	Argirades	Perivolion	Lefkimmi	Kavos
06.30**	07.05**	07.20**	07.35**	07.50**	08.10**
08.30*	08.05*	08.20*	08.35*	08.50*	09.10*
09.30	10.05	10.20	10.35	10.50	11.10
10.30*	11.05*	11.20*	11.35*	11.50*	12.10*
11.30**	12.05**	12.20**	12.35**	12.50**	13.10**
12.30*	13.05*	13.20*	13.35*	13.50*	14.10*
13.30**	14.05**	14.20**	14.35**	14.50**	15.10**
15.30***	16.05***	16.20***	16.35***	16.50***	17.10***
17.30***	18.05***	18.20***	18.35***	18.50***	19.10***
19.30	20.05	20.20	20.35	20.50	21.10

*not Saturday or Sunday; **not Sunday; ***departs 30min earlier on Sundays

RETURN BUSES

Kavos	Lefkimmi	Perivolion	Argirades	Messongi	Corfu
07.50**	08.10**	08.25**	08.40**	08.55**	09.30**
10.00*	10.20*	10.35*	10.50*	11.05*	11.40*
11.00	11.20	11.35	11.50	12.05	12.40
12.00*	12.20*	12.35*	12.50*	13.05*	13.40*
13.50*	14.10*	14.25*	14.40*	14.45*	15.20*
14.00*	14.20*	14.35*	14.50*	15.05*	15.40*
15.00**	15.20**	15.35**	15.50**	16.05**	16.40**
17.00***	17.20***	17.35***	17.50***	18.05***	18.40***
19.00**	19.20**	19.35**	19.50**	20.05**	20.40**
21.00	21.20	21.35	21.50	22.05	22.40

*not Saturday or Sunday; **not Sunday; ***departs 30min earlier on Sundays

3 Corfu • Benitses • Messongi

		Monday to Saturday			
Corfu	Benitses	Messongi	Messongi	Benitses	Corfu
09.00	09.25	09.40	07.15	07.30	07.55
11.30	11.55	12.15	08.30	08.45	09.10
12.00	12.25	12.40	09.45	10.00	10.25
14.30	14.55	15.10	12.45	13.00	13.25
15.30	15.55	16.10	16.00	16.15	16.40
17.30	17.55	18.10	18.45	19.00	19.25
18.30	18.55	19.10	19.15	19.30	19.55
		Sundays and holidays			
10.00	10.25	10.40	10.15	10.30	10.55
			18.15	18.30	18.55

4 Corfu • Sinarades (via Kastellani) • Ag Gordis

		Monday to Saturday			
Corfu	Sinarades	Ag Gordis	Ag Gordis	Sinarades	Corfu
08.15	08.45	08.55	09.00	09.10	09.40
09.15	09.45	09.55	10.00	10.10	10.40
14.30	15.00	15.10	11.30	11.40	12.10
17.30	18.00	18.10	15.15	15.25	15.55
			18.15	18.25	19.05
			20.00	20.30	20.40
		Sundays and holidays			
09.30	09.55	10.00	10.15	10.25	10.55
17.30	18.00	18.10	18.15	18.25	18.55

5 Corfu • Vatos (via Ag Ioannis) • Glyfada

Monday to Saturday			Sundays and holidays		
Corfu	Vatos	Glyfada	Corfu	Vatos	Glyfada
06.45	07.15	07.25	09.00	09.30	09.40
09.00	09.30	09.40	11.00	11.30	11.40
11.00	11.30	11.40	13.00	13.30	13.40
14.00	14.30	14.40	16.00	16.30	16.40
16.00	16.30	16.40			
20.00	20.30	20.40			

RETURN BUSES

Monday to Saturday			Sundays and holidays		
Glyfada	Vatos	Corfu	Glyfada	Vatos	Corfu
07.15	07.25	07.55	09.45	09.55	10.25
10.00	10.10	10.40	11.45	11.55	12.25
11.45	11.55	12.25	13.45	13.55	14.25
14.45	14.55	15.25	16.45	16.55	17.25
16.45	16.55	17.25			
20.45	20.55	21.15			

6 Corfu • Ermones • Corfu

Daily. Departs Corfu 07.40, 09.30, 14.30, 19.00; returns from Ermones 07.35, 10.05, 15.05, 19.35; journey time 35min.

7 Corfu • Ag Georgios Beach (near Argirades)

Monday to Saturday		Sundays and holidays	
Corfu	Ag Georgios	Corfu	Ag Georgios
09.30	10.30	10.00	11.00
15.30	16.30	16.00	17.00
17.30	18.30		

RETURN BUSES

Ag Georgios	Corfu	Ag Georgios	Corfu
10.00	11.00	10.45	11.45
16.30	17.30	18.15	19.15
18.30	19.30		

8 Corfu • Arkadades • Sidari • Peroulades • Avliotes • Ag Stefanos

		Monday to Friday			
Corfu	Arkadades	Sidari	Peroulades	Avliotes	Ag Stefanos
05.45	06.25	06.55	07.00	07.10	07.15
09.00	09.40	10.10	10.15	10.25	10.35
14.00	14.40	15.10	15.15	15.25	15.35
15.45	16.25	16.55	17.00	17.10	17.15
19.30	20.10	20.40	20.45	20.55	21.05
		Saturday			
09.00	09.40	10.10	10.15	10.25	10.35
13.30	14.10	14.40	14.45	14.55	15.05
15.45	16.25	16.55	17.00	17.10	17.20
19.30	20.10	20.40	20.45	20.55	21.05
	Sundays and holidays — only one bus				
09.30	10.10	10.40	10.45	10.55	11.05

RETURN BUSES

		Monday to Friday			
Ag Stefanos	Avliotes	Peroulades	Sidari	Arkadades	Corfu
07.00	07.10	07.20	07.25	07.55	08.35
10.30	10.40	10.50	10.55	11.25	12.05
15.30	15.40	15.50	15.55	16.25	17.05
17.45	17.55	18.25	18.30	19.00	19.40
21.10	21.20	21.30	21.35	22.05	22.45
		Saturday			
07.00	07.10	07.20	07.25	07.55	08.35
10.30	10.40	10.50	10.55	11.25	12.05

Ag Stefanos	Avliotes	Peroulades	Sidari	Arkadades	Corfu
15.30	15.40	15.50	15.55	15.25	16.05
17.45	17.55	18.05	18.10	18.40	19.20
21.10	21.20	21.30	21.35	22.05	22.45
		Sundays and holidays — only one bus			
17.00	17.10	17.20	17.25	17.55	18.35

9 Corfu • Troumpeta • Khoroepiskopi • Roda • Acharavi

Corfu	Troumpeta	Khoroepiskopi	Roda	Acharavi
		Monday to Friday		
05.45	06.15	06.25	06.45	07.00
09.15	09.45	09.55	10.15	10.30
13.45	14.15	14.25	14.45	15.00
16.00	16.30	16.40	17.00	17.15
		Saturday		
05.45	06.15	06.25	06.45	07.00
09.15	09.45	09.55	10.15	10.30
14.00	14.30	14.40	15.00	15.15
16.00	16.30	16.40	17.00	17.15
		Sundays and holidays — only one bus		
09.30	10.00	10.10	10.30	10.45

RETURN BUSES
Monday to Saturday

Acharavi	Roda	Khoroepiskopi	Troumpeta	Corfu
07.15	07.30	07.50	08.00	08.30
10.30	10.15	10.35	10.45	11.15
15.30	15.45	16.05	16.15	16.45
17.15	17.30	17.50	18.00	18.30
		Sundays and holidays — only one bus		
17.15	17.30	17.50	18.00	18.30

10 Corfu • Magoulades • Afionas

Monday to Friday only*

Corfu	Magoulades	Afionas	Arilas	Afionas	Arilas	Magoulades	Corfu
05.45	06.50	07.10	07.25	06.45	07.00	07.10	08.15
13.45	15.50	16.10	16.25	15.15	15.30	15.40	16.45

*On Saturdays there is one bus: departs Corfu at 13.30; returns from Afionas at 15.30

11 Corfu • Nissaki • Kalami turn-off • Kassiopi • Perithia • Loutses

Monday to Saturday

Corfu	Nissaki	Kalami turn-off	Ag Stephanos turn-off	Kassiopi	Perithia	Loutses
05.45	06.25	06.40	06.45	06.50	07.00	07.05
09.00	09.40	09.55	10.00	10.05	10.15	
10.00	10.40	10.55	11.00	11.05	11.15	
12.15	12.55	13.10	13.15	13.20	13.30	
14.30	15.10	15.25	15.30	15.35	15.45	15.50
16.00	16.40	16.55	17.00	17.05	17.20	
		Sundays and holidays — one bus only				
09.30	10.10	10.25	10.30	10.35	10.45	

RETURN BUSES
Monday to Saturday

Loutses	Perithia	Kassiopi	Ag Stephanos turn-off	Kalami turn-off	Nissaki	Corfu
07.15	07.20	07.30	07.35	07.40	07.55	08.35
	10.20	10.25	10.30	10.35	10.50	11.30
	11.05	11.15	11.20	11.25	12.40	13.20
	13.20	13.30	13.35	13.40	14.55	15.35
16.00	16.05	16.15	16.20	16.25	16.40	17.20
		Sundays and holidays — one bus only				
17.00	17.05	17.15	17.20	17.25	17.40	18.20

12 Corfu • Pyrgi/Ipsos

Monday to Saturday*		Sundays and holidays	
Corfu	**Pyrgi/Ipsos**	**Corfu**	**Pyrgi/Ipsos**
07.00	07.00	09.30	10.00
09.00	09.00	12.00	12.30
09.30	10.00	17.30	18.00
12.00	12.30		
14.00	14.30		
15.30	16.00		
17.00	17.30		
18.30	19.00		
20.00	20.00		

*No 15.30 service; last bus 19.30

RETURN BUSES

Monday to Saturday*		Sundays and holidays	
Pyrgi/Ipsos	**Corfu**	**Pyrgi/Ipsos**	**Corfu**
07.30	08.00	09.50	10.20
09.30	10.00	12.30	13.00
10.30	11.00	17.50	18.20
12.30	13.00		
14.30	15.00		
16.00	16.30		
17.45	18.15		
19.15	19.45		
20.00	20.00		

*On Saturdays the 10.30 bus leaves at 10.45, the 17.30 bus at 17.45 and there is no service at 16.00.

13 Kassiopi • Roda • Sidari

Monday to Saturday, and public holidays, but no service on Sunday					
Kassiopi	**Roda**	**Sidari**	**Sidari**	**Roda**	**Kassiopi**
09.30	09.55	10.15	10.15	10.35	11.00
11.15	11.40	12.00	12.00	12.20	12.45
14.30	14.55	15.15	15.15	15.35	16.00
16.00	16.25	16.45	16.45	17.05	17.30